HEINEMANN
SCHOOL
MANAGEMENT

Marketing the School

MICHAEL MARLAND
AND   RICK ROGERS

Heinemann Educational
A division of Heinemann Educational Books Ltd.,
Halley Court, Jordan Hill, Oxford OX2 8EJ

OXFORD LONDON EDINBURGH
MADRID ATHENS BOLOGNA PARIS
MELBOURNE SYDNEY AUCKLAND SINGAPORE TOKYO
IBADAN NAIROBI HARARE GABORONE
PORTSMOUTH NH (USA)

A catalogue record for this book is available from the British Library

ISBN 0-435-80596-7
Produced by **AMR Ltd**
Printed in England by Clays Ltd., St Ives plc

Acknowledgements

The authors and publishers would like to thank the following for permission
to use material:

Bicester Community College (Figs. 5, 6, 8); British Rail (Fig. 3);
Cadbury's Ltd (Fig. 3); Crestwood School (Figs. 4, 9); Heart of England Sixth
Form Centre (Fig. 9); Midland Bank PLC (Fig. 3); Newham Community
College (Fig. 1); North Westminster Community School (Figs. 2, 4, 10, 11, 12);
Reception conversion designed by Culum and Nightingale, 61 Judd Street,
London WC1H 9QT (Fig. 11); St Clement Danes Primary School (Fig. 7);
The Body Shop PLC (Fig. 3); Virgin Atlantic Airways (Fig. 3);
Wycliffe College (Fig. 8)

Index compiled by Indexing Specialists, Hove, Sussex.

Printed in Great Britain by Athenæum Press Ltd, Newcastle upon Tyne
94 95 96 97 98   10 9 8 7 6 5 4 3 2

Contents

Preface

The aim of *Marketing the School* is to provide schools with an essential tool for the future in which schools will be more independent and able to shape themselves. There is a greater public interest in and concern for schooling than ever before. Developments such as open enrolment, parents' right to more detailed information about school performance, the option of grant-maintained status, and the local management of schools mean that governing bodies and Headteachers will have to be expert in promoting their school.

However, the purpose is wider than that: good marketing can help to give parents, pupils, the local community, education officials, and local business an accurate and positive profile of a school. The skills needed for this can range from knowing how to handle a critical report in the local press to developing a corporate identity for the whole school.

Marketing the School is written to provide Headteachers, senior staff, and governors with information and advice on a wide range of issues, so as to enable them to make the most of the school and its activities. The book will serve as a handy reference for one-off situations, and a detailed guide to longer-term planning, and it also seeks to relate marketing to school management as a whole.

The focus of this book is clearly important for both schooling in general and individual schools. Schools need to present themselves and their work more vigorously and imaginatively than ever before if they are to gain the fullest public support.

The concepts, techniques, and examples included in this book are drawn from experience across the country. However, I have not hesitated to use my own experience as a Head of two schools.

This experience has included an acute case of needing to create an identity and a favourable image: opening a new school as its Head. Three schools were closed in 1980, none of which was attracting either sufficient pupils in number or range of abilities. For years there had been arguments about the best way forward, whilst the three schools declined still further under a planning blight. We had to create a new school in the face of public distrust of the old ones and dismay at the complexity of a three-site school. 'No mother worth her salt,' declared one local resident to me, 'would send her daughter to *that* school'!

Such a challenge absolutely required 'marketing': 'no pupils' equals 'no school' and a much impoverished school for those pupils unlucky enough to be enrolled.

Whilst I can see in retrospect many things could have been done better, and some that we missed altogether, we succeeded in building up to a full and fully balanced intake of pupils within three years. Of course, this would not have been possible without the best possible planning and delivery of pastoral care and the curriculum. However, it also depended on the projection and promotion of what we had to offer and what we were achieving. Marketing is partly about attracting pupils, but it is also to do with raising awareness and improving regard and self-esteem in everyone's minds, including pupils and parents already in the school.

This book is a collaboration with Rick Rogers, who has written three chapters from his expertise in freelance journalism, and contributed to others throughout the book. We should both like to thank the many people with whom we have worked, and the schools and organisations whose experience we have drawn on.

London, 1991

1 Marketing and the role of the school

The popular view is that 'marketing' is a gloss given to something that is already established and is often little affected by the marketing exercise. More than that, it is seen as separate, and only artificially connected to what is being marketed. Indeed, many would presume that marketing is not only a process of exaggerating, but probably is frequently dishonest.

The argument of this book is the converse: to increase knowledge about a school and to promote its image among its clients – that is parents as well as pupils – and the communities it serves is not a gloss but is *integral* to the work of the school. Indeed, to enhance community esteem requires self-evaluation, and both strengthen the work of the school in all its aspects.

■ Marketing and management

An important aspect of the 'marketing' concept is what it does to the determination to deliver what is promised. The great writer Primo Levi tells, in *The Periodic Table,* his memoirs of the years after his release from Auschwitz when, as a trained chemist, he returns to work in senior positions in a chemical factory. He moves to a job in Customers' Service, and reflects on it as I should reflect on the analogous marketing of a school:

> ▶ 'To perform it with success you must infuse faith in customers, and therefore it is indispensable to have faith in yourself and in the products you sell; it is therefore a salutary activity, which helps you to know yourself and strengthens your character.'

You cannot market the indefensible; you cannot 'infuse faith' if you do not have faith in your school's work yourself. You cannot have that faith if you do not 'know yourself'. So, marketing starts with analysis of the working of the school, a self-audit without which external promotion is simply not possible.

This means that the marketing of the school leads inevitably to ensuring that the promises made are kept and that weaknesses are tackled. Marketing is not a mere cosmetic activity to be entered into cynically, but one that is integral to self-evaluation and continuous development.

With the clarification of power and the redistribution of it in the Acts of 1986 and 1988, the governors are now the node of power. This allows a much greater degree of internal management: schools can now use their delegated budget to shape, present, and manage the workings of their school in the way that seems right for that school. Thus marketing should be seen as the corollary of internal management.

■ Marketing and parents

All of us in schools see the value of education and perhaps take it for granted that others will readily do so. We perhaps forget that there is a range of somewhat questioning attitudes amongst people not employed in schools, and that these attitudes can be held by well-meaning, knowledgeable, and concerned people. Not all critics are fools or knaves.

First, the law (specifically the *Education Act 1944*) makes *parents* responsible for educating their children: if a family can make adequate arrangements they need not use schools. Parents are thus *clients* and schools their *agents* in fulfilling their obligation. True it is only the rare parent who makes other arrangements, but the perspective opened by the possibility is an important one for understanding the role of a school.

There are many parents and other members of the communities we serve who have legitimately unhappy memories of their own schools, and whose criticisms of past school failures are accurate and fair. Furthermore, many of the current criticisms of our work are also fair, albeit we may have adequate explanations citing lack of resources and support. As in many areas of life, the wash-over of the past or present deficiencies can sully that which is good and could change views.

■ Parents and the professionals

Possibly our worst fault is that which I call 'professio-centricism' – the conscious or unconscious attitude that the qualified teacher knows so much that the views of others are at best irrelevant, and almost certainly inaccurate. This was epitomised by the Headteacher of a London junior school in the mid-seventies, Terry Ellis, who said in the witness box at the enquiry into William Tyndale School: 'Parents, don't talk to me about parents; we're the pros in this business.'

In the United Kingdom, we have historically and habitually kept parents 'at arm's length'. We have asked parents to 'support the school', and often criticised them because they 'supported the child'. There has been a gradual, though intermittent, move towards greater responsiveness towards parents and to giving them greater power.

It is very often forgotten that the law makes parents the clients of the school. Alastair Macbeth sets this out clearly in his book *Involving Parents*. It is a crucial point for school management and marketing:

▶ **'Education authorities are required by Section 7 of the 1944 Act to make educational facilities available. We may pose the question: for what purpose? If parents are responsible for their child's education, then the facilities must exist to assist parents in carrying out their legal duty. In brief, parents may be seen as the school's prime legal clients, until the child is 16 years of age.'**

Despite the protestations of most of us working in schools that our schools relate well to parents, the evidence is clear that:

- compared with most schools in European Community countries we have fewer parental contacts;

- a huge proportion of parents feel out of touch and under-involved in their child's schooling;

- very many teachers, much of the time, are ignorant or misinformed about their pupils' homes, and their concerns and expectations;

- over the years since the war, a variety of forces have led to an unconsultative approach, in which innovations, aspects of the curriculum, and school procedures have been approached either with insufficient thought for the views of families or merely for the sake of professional aims.

It is interesting to untangle the strands that led by, say the end of the seventies, to this professio-centric approach: the boarding-school tradition of 'choosing the best school and leave it to them'; the class patronisation of the grammar school; the general sense of rescuing unfortunates of the secondary modern school; and the unconscious or even overt racism that belittles families of minority ethnic background.

Underlying all this was the typical post-war elevation of a profession (as happened to town planners, doctors, engineers, and accountants) in order to create the new world. Many in teaching voiced the view that only 'qualified teachers' should express ideas about the work of the school: governors, industrialists, the DES and, certainly, parents, should 'leave it to the professionals'.

The Plowden Report on primary schools in 1967 marked an official change of attitude towards parents. The days of notices that 'Parents should not come beyond this point' were numbered.

■ A new partnership for our schools

In particular, the 'client-led' revolution that moved across the world and through society brought all professionals from behind the veil of their specialism to answer to the lay person. Teachers and education were slow to respond. The Taylor Report of 1977, '*A New Partnership for Our Schools*', re-considered the government of schools and made a strong case for greater formal parental participation. A decade later, the 1986 Act brought greater parental influence into the enhanced power of the governing body.

The eighties saw the gradual extension of research studies demonstrating the educational value of home-school partnership. Starting with children with medical or learning difficulties, regimes planned jointly were successful in a variety of settings. Greatly enhanced reading scores could be obtained by parents and teachers working together. Indeed, the amateur who merely listened regularly to a child read, could enhance the reading as much as a teacher.

Others found that there was far more parental support in many parts of society than had been thought. One study of infant school children showed that there was more, and more complex, oral interchange at home than in school! More generally, the broad class-school success correlation was being broken up to show that it was not just social class that determined a pupil's attainment level, but significantly the support that was being offered by homes. This could be inhibited or increased by the attitudes, procedures, and presentation of schools.

For general societal and specific school reasons, society was, therefore, gradually changing:

- all members of society were demanding more openness from professionals;

- dissatisfaction with schooling was being voiced by a wide variety of people;

- new research was leading to a position where the contribution of parents was being spelt out.

Recent legislation has formally expressed this new combination of attitudes in a series of procedures, from the place of parents on the governing body, to the annual governors' report to parents. In particular, schools must now provide detailed information to parents.

This post-eighties dispensation makes schools more responsive to parents and creates a more balanced partnership. Commenting on the under-powered structures, management, and resources of schools, Marten Shipman said in his contribution 'The Limits of Positive Discrimination' in *Education for the Inner City* in 1980:

▶ **'A way forward would be to strike a bargain between parents and teachers. Parents would offer more support and receive more power to affect decisions about central issues such as the curriculum. Teachers would yield some of their professional autonomy in exchange for support. This would require a major effort of mass communication to spell out the benefits that could accrue.'**

Thus marketing can be seen as part of power-sharing with parents.

■ Marketing and competition

In many parts of the country schools now compete for pupils. The *Education Act 1981* was the main legislative expression of this, and it defined more widely than ever before the right of parents to *choose* a school for their children. This was seen for some years as part of the then Conservative government's political stance. However, it would also be true to observe that parents had long wanted this right and in many places, particularly densely populated city areas, exercised it as far as they could. For instance, in the centre of London, with its complex public transport system, parents, in the years since the war, had fought against the attempts of the London County Council and Inner London Education Authority to rationalise transfer to secondary schools.

The obvious and major problem with competition is the harm it does to the less publicly attractive school. Before a school 'goes to the wall', it endures a protracted period in which declining rolls and declining confidence make the delivery of a full and varied education to the pupils still there much harder.

However, in many areas the 'standard number' legislation of the

Education Act (No.2) 1986 combined with the 'school choice' legislation of 1981 has led to more openly direct competition. However, this has its advantages, and it is worth pointing out that some LEAs (especially in large cities) were unable to prevent the drift to popular schools in the seventies and eighties. Schools whose declining numbers were weakening the standard of education being offered had little power with which to tackle their plight. Now they can use the competitive situation to hold their position, or even improve it with or without 'opting out'.

Each school will wish to collaborate and consult with its neighbours, and must then decide the professional ethic of marketing in order to compete for pupils. There will be times when co-operation will be right, but undoubtedly times when a school will already have felt the brunt of LEA schemes that have favoured other schools.

However, what has to be accepted as an irreversible shift of parent/school relationships is that, when transport permits, parents will choose. One part of marketing will be addressed to competition. There is no ignoring this aspect of school management in the future: marketing will be an essential component of school leadership.

■ Conclusion

The overall task of school marketing is to provide hard information in an appropriate style, which will enable parents to see how the school can fulfil the educational needs of their children. The LEA's – the providers – and pupils and their parents – the users – need to receive a clear and well presented view of what the school has to offer. Thus, a sound approach to marketing enhances the quality of all aspects of the central service offered by the LEA to the institution itself: it attracts pupils to the school; it elicits parental enthusiasm when they are there; and it gains wider community support. School management is woven through with marketing.

2 Planning a coherent programme

Both teaching and marketing require effective communication and presentation. There is no mystique about marketing skills. However, on the one hand the traditions, restricted resources, and desperate lack of time have reduced the emphasis on presentation required by schools for the prime task of educating its pupils. On the other hand, many of those who come in to teaching are not naturally skilful writers or speakers and there is little or no in-service work on communication skills. Schools are often institutions in which notices, circulars, and worksheets are badly drafted, poorly designed, and erratically reproduced.

■ Why plan?

The Local Management aspect of the 1988 legislation on education has given schools the opportunity to plan themselves as a whole and meet *our* school's aims in *our* way.

Even the most publicity-conscious schools of the past have tended to approach their marketing task in a fragmented way: a gesture here, an event there, and a publication redesigned once in a while. At their best, these schools allowed opportunity to prompt action. Usually there was no one with co-ordinating responsibility for publicity, and no coherent relationship between a school's aims and its public relations and marketing.

Ideally, the marketing role should be planned into the structure of the school, and should not be conceived as a virtually separate 'system', nor so disseminated that everyone has some responsibility but no one co-ordinates.

Before an appropriate responsibility pattern can be devised, it is worth considering the theoretical aspects of marketing: Of what does it consist?

■ The four phases of marketing

Theoretically, marketing has four phases:

client research;
product development;
promotion;
quality control.

This technical analysis of the commercial world is not as remote or alien as it may at first appear, and it is worth considering the relationship between these marketing concepts and schooling. The phrases might have the ring of commerce, but the processes they describe are realistic for virtually all organisations, and certainly for schools.

■ Client research

Our stance tends to be that as professionals, trained (albeit, compared to e.g. lawyers or doctors, very skimpily) and experienced and working within national legislation and National Curriculum requirements, we know what we should offer, and we know what it is that the pupils and their families require.

There is, of course, a great deal of truth in this: much education remains unassailable by popularity or parental preference: the truth of a scientific hypothesis or the appropriateness of a language pattern are virtually absolute. However, we have tended to extend the boundaries of what is strictly 'true' and professionally necessary well beyond that. We have failed to enrich our school life or our professional repertoire by finding out what *others* think about schooling and what *they* want for it. Even if we disagree and declare 'We'll have none of that', it is necessary for us to know that what we do and say really is believed.

Often, though, we can genuinely learn, especially from parents. Thus, the idea of 'market research' (developed more fully in the chapter on page 27) is useful to school planning.

■ Product development

It is uncomfortable to think of schooling as a 'product', as that word has been given limited and perjorative associations. In fact, though, its meaning is appropriate to schools. A product is that created by producing – that is to lead (*'duc'*) forward (*'pro'*). A product is that which results from creative planning, and 'product development' in this context is, therefore, the work of the school in establishing what would benefit the pupils and researching and planning it.

One useful aspect of the concept of 'product development' in schooling is that, for the time being, it divides 'delivery' (teaching or tutoring) from *what* is being taught and *how* it is taught. Hitherto, schools have been under-managed internally. The ratio of 'planning' or 'development' to 'delivery' is unsatisfactory. The assumption tends to be that schooling *is* teaching a full class. The in-school curriculum development is rushed, very limited, and under prepared. Similarly, schools have had very little planning opportunity for pastoral care.

In schools 'product development' is the jargon shorthand for the *preparation*, without which the skill of the staff is being under-used. 'Marketing' can help to formulate an understanding of what is required and then help to plan it.

■ Promotion

If 'product development' lies uncomfortably on the tongue of educators, so does 'promotion'. But why? It is only the idea of 'putting forward' the work of the school. There is no escaping the fact that a school's work is viewed and judged by pupils, staff, parents, and the communities it serves. It is part of the school's work to assist this process, both by making knowledge available, and by the way that information is selected, shaped, and presented.

■ Quality control

This is probably the least acceptable of the four concepts, perhaps because we do not like to face the possibility that our work is less than perfect. As every part of the profession moves to an acceptance of some form of appraisal, no doubt we shall formalise methods of monitoring all aspects of the work of the school, *by* the school and *for* the school's planning. The corollary of local management is in-school scrutiny, and the allocation of resources to improve that which needs improving.

Thus the four phases of marketing are integral and cyclical: one leading to the next and the last back again to the beginning, and each a crucial part of school management.

■ SWOT analysis

When a school is planning a 'marketing' programme, SWOT is useful as a tool with which to appraise the internal and external factors that affect and influence the school's performance.

This is a well-recognised commercial marketing term. The acronym stands for:

internal Strengths and Weaknesses and external Opportunities and Threats

When the school looks at what a business would call a 'marketing audit' it might consider these factors.

■ Internal Strengths and Weaknesses

What does the school do well and what does it not do so well? Such an analysis might, for instance, find pastoral care and sport or drama as strengths and academic achievement as a weakness. This analysis recognises where targets may need improving, without in any way downgrading those aspects of the school of which it should be justly proud – it may even upgrade them. By facing this analysis of strengths and weaknesses, the school gives itself another opportunity to improve itself.

■ External Opportunities and Threats

Here the school can assess all those factors which might be used as 'reasons and excuses' for inaction: the economic, political, or social environment may hold the school back or cause it to struggle. The total 'market' may well be falling in some areas as a community dwindles or ages, but in other areas the community may be burgeoning, and yet this may not be recognised by the school's policy makers.

A school should look seriously at its 'market share' in the face of competition and, without ever criticising other schools, consider how it can meet them fairly. Often the competition is not from other all-age schools (even between single sex and mixed schools), but between the school and the Sixth Form College option which creams off the top age group. Can the age group be retained in the face of such competition or may the school be more comfortable without them?

Some of the factors considered by a SWOT analysis in a business may not be relevant to the school, but using such an analysis can help a school plan for the future.

■ Internal management

There is an inevitable tension between devising a marketing scheme which is sufficiently coherent (so that, for instance, the logo does not change from one version to another) and one which is sufficiently flexible (so that, for instance, a Head of Department may contact the local press direct). The best balance will have to be devised to suit the school, its style, its area, and its size.

Further Education Colleges have had considerably more and larger experience of marketing than schools, especially as they have always had to seek students for their courses (Figure 1 shows such a prospectus). For instance, each of the Hertfordshire colleges has a 'Marketing Co-ordinator', whose role is described by Robin Shreeve and Jane Thorp in their *Marketing Hertfordshire Colleges*:

> ▶ **'The role of the College Marketing Co-ordinator is to market effectively the college's complete range of services with emphasis on seeking out new education and training business and to co-ordinate the marketing efforts of college staff.**
>
> **Marketing is seen as a whole-college activity. The Marketing Co-ordinator will need to work with college management in encouraging the development of a responsive service at all levels in colleges. This includes the caretaker and the receptionists as well as lecturers and Heads of Department.'**

Often this responsibility is carried by a Vice Principal, using the central office services as the clerical resource. Such a person has to solicit ideas from Heads of Department and has to co-ordinate the input of a range of middle management to the brochures and advertisements. To this end, all the middle-management responsibility holders must have this expectation built into *their* job specifications.

Figure 1 Further Education College prospectus

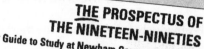

THE PROSPECTUS OF THE NINETEEN-NINETIES
Your Guide to Study at Newham Community College

Starting Out
If you're thinking of leaving school this year, or have recently left, and you're not quite sure of what to do next, we can help. There are many ways to a good career through part-time or full-time study. Find out about starting out at Newham Community College.

 2-3

Changing Direction
Are you stuck in a rut? Or worse, are you facing the prospect of redundancy? Do you need to retrain to better your prospects, or do you feel it's time you expanded your horizons and extended yourself? There are lots of opportunities to change direction.

 4-5

Moving Forward
You're established in your career and you're ambitious to go further. You need to know the route through to management and professional status. College qualifications can be gained in a variety of ways.

 6-7

g Your Workforce
or corporate success in the nineties.
nces or a multinational company,
keep up to date and keep ahead.

 8-9

Starting Afresh
me to ease back into education?
begin again in informal, learning
with your convenience in mind.

 10

Out of Interest
range of interest courses in the
uld never find time to be bored!

 11

rting the Student
n keeping up with the syllabus.
s and help with your problems.

 12

how Newham Community College
s of serving the whole community.
u, find out more about the courses
Community Education Directory,
acks of course information sheets.
ain subject areas for convenience.
rmation on the courses it includes.
ever packs are of interest to you.

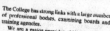

The College has strong links with a large number of professional bodies, examining boards and training agencies.

We are a major provider of Higher National awards, Advanced Craft and Professional qualifications in Business subjects, the Building Industry, Construction and Engineering crafts, Catering, Laboratory Science, Graphic Design, Electronics, Computing and Management Training.

▅▅ Who should be the Marketing Co-ordinator?

Schools obviously face a choice: the marketing task could be given to:

- a freelance person (perhaps a parent);
- in a large school, a full-time administrator, responsible for all school publications;
- a senior administrator (e.g. Director of Communications, if the school is large enough to have one) as part of his or her job;
- a senior teacher (e.g. one of the Deputy Heads);
- a teacher, with release time and an appropriate Incentive Allowance;
- the Headteacher, perhaps with the Chair of Governors, especially in a small school.

There are, of course, advantages and disadvantages to each. The crucial balance is between seniority and availability. In a sense, the Head is inevitably involved in so many external public relations jobs that only she or he can do that there is sense in the Head being the co-ordinator. On the other hand, the burden and pressure on the Head might be too great for proper oversight.

In a large enough school the best solution is probably for an experienced teacher with the right skills and interests to have an appropriate proportion of release time for the role.

▅▅ How to manage the task

Some parts of the work have to be reduced to routine if possible, for if every task is devised afresh, the effort and time involved get out of proportion. Annual mailings, booklet production, and advertising campaigns can be planned, trialled, and then made routine. In this way, year after year, the cycle is run through, without the great expense of trauma and money that fresh starts demand.

However, if parts of the marketing programme become too routine and are not looked at from one year to the next, they are likely to become dated and let down the rest of the programme. It is important, therefore, to reconsider them annually, even if no changes are then made. This is one example of the importance of 'quality control'.

Whatever decisions about structure are made, the Head will have to be interested and considerably involved, for the marketing of the school, as we have seen, is creating the voice of the school, and the leader of the school must contribute to that voice and feel comfortable with it.

■ How to create the overall plan

It is unlikely that many schools will need to agree detailed plans, and there will always be scope for extemporising. However, it is worth while having at least a loose plan. This will come from the 'four phases' described on pages 8-9 in the light of the formal aims of the school and the findings of the research described in Chapter 4 (pages 27-33).

Whether explicit or implicit, the first stage must be to build a picture of the school which identifies its special features and its benefits. This is not an activity that comes naturally to schools, where the defensive mode is too often triggered by ill-informed criticism on the one hand and inadequate resources on the other.

However, whilst 'product development' and a school 'development plan' should continue to work on weaker aspects as part of longer-term development, for the initial marketing plan immediate realism is crucial. If your school's home/school liaison is rather weak, you cannot promote it as a special feature. If your sports record is patchy, there is no point highlighting it just yet.

Some of the techniques described under **Client Research** (pages 27-33) are useful. This self-scrutiny is carried out in a somewhat different way from the objective study, as part of a thorough development plan: this unashamedly identifies the good features.

The results should be put against an objective survey of buildings, grounds, activities, and performance indicators. The strongest of these should be extracted and listed.

Finally, the aims of the school as established by the governors under the terms of Section 18 of the *Education Act (No2) 1986* should be culled for the key ambitions.

From this exercise comes an analytic map of the marketable features of the school. This may have existed already in some people's minds, but it needs drawing out and listing clearly as the first step of the plan.

Secondly, the result of the research on client needs, however informally carried out, should be used as a check against the findings of the 'offer': what is sought that is currently really on offer? Here is the core of what is to be highlighted. The school's message is derived from that analysis.

■ How to put the message across

The complementary mapping is of the ways of putting that message across: the most readily thought of are often called 'the media', though, as I hope to show, that phrase is unnecessarily limiting as it normally includes only the news/entertainment media of press, radio, and television and specific advertisements. Yet schools have other possibilities also.

Conventional publicity manuals are not geared to schools, and, not surprisingly, overlook those opportunities that are particular to a school. It is possible to list on a chart the key features of the school and against each the promotional media most likely to suit. I am not suggesting that there will be a one-to-one correlation between school aspect and promotion output, but that the overall plan essentially places publicity opportunities against the attributes map.

However, it is true that some areas of the media suit some aspects of the school better than others: news outlets suit 'events', because events are a 'newspeg', rather than 'qualities' (like good home/school liaison); school publications, on the other hand, can convey many aspects of the aspirations and achievements of pupils.

It is unlikely that a school would wish to, or be able to, use all possibilities each year, but the overall plan needs to take them all into account. Sometimes chance will suggest one rather than another; at other times the nature of the idea will clearly suit one possibility rather than another. Yet again, though, the range of possibilities should be reviewed from time to time and possibilities followed up. The overall plan will take into account different aspects of the school and the promotional opportunities available.

■ Marketing and school services

As the prime task of schools is educating their pupils of statutory age, other 'saleable offers' should be and must be limited. Nevertheless, any such services that can be marketed have a place in the overall plan, both to gain revenue and to offer a service to the community.

With the legislation of 1986 and 1988, a school is free to hire out its buildings and facilities, sell its print technology, its teaching skills, and its knowledge. For most schools the buildings and grounds can legitimately be rented out for a variety of purposes.

Obviously, these services have to be marketed, however modestly. The hiring out, say, of the school hall can bring in useful income if it is properly costed to incorporate all overheads, including the time of the staff negotiating the letting. The most appropriate mix of methods will be chosen as part of the overall plan, even if it is no more than an advertisement in the local paper or a simple brochure.

Two points, though, relate to the overall marketing of the school and we should bear in mind that the marketing of the services should not be regarded as entirely separate:

- Whatever the vehicle chosen to advertise the service being offered, it should be also seen as carrying the *school's* central message. The higher the regard for the school, the more saleable the service, and vice versa. Thus a leaflet about the rooms available for hire can readily carry brief copy about the achievements of the school.

- Any event run in hired school premises can also be an advertising vehicle for the school. For instance, a disu.nguished national choir hires one of the North Westminster School halls for its rehearsals. The programme at its public performances at concert venues carries (as part of the hire contract) the advertisement shown in Figure 2.

Many schools seek to hire out their premises and their staff and sell some of their products and services. The judicious marketing of these can also promote the central work of the school.

St. John's Smith Square
Westminster, London SW1   Director: Paul Davies

Sunday, 21st October
at 7.30 p.m.

Purcell O Sing unto the Lord a new song

Handel Dixit Dominus

Bach Brandenburg Concerto No.3

Mozart Missa Brevis KV275

Ana Maria Rincón & Bridget Corderoy *sopranos*   Adèle Paxton *contralto*
Paul Badley *tenor*   Karl Morgan *bass*

English Baroque Choir
English Baroque Players
Leader: Diana Cummings
Conductor: LEON LOVETT

Violins
Diana Cummings
David Ogden
Michael de Saulles
Lisa Polunin

Violas
Christopher Wellington
Elizabeth Watson
Lisa Polunin

Violoncelli
Marilyn Sansom
Andrea Hess

Double Bass
Roy Chilton

Chamber Organ   Stephen Jones

Concert and Orchestra Manager:
͏‑‑‑‑side, London NW7 2LJ Tel: 081-959 2688

He͏

The E͏

͏‑‑‑‑ncial support

ST JOHN'S SMITH S͏
Director: Paul Davi͏

For details of future ev͏
In accordance with the͏
stand in any gangway.͏
den without formal c͏

Arts at School
The English Baroque Choir rehearses at North
Westminster Community School in Marylebone,
and we are pleased to support them.
With a Studio Theatre (opened by Jessye
Norman), close connections with the Royal Opera
House and the City of Westminster Arts Council,
excellent arts facilities, and a strong department
of Visual Arts and Performing Arts, we always
welcome pupils keen on extending their artistic
skills.
There's a range of courses for older students in
Upper School in music, dance, drama, stage
management, and visual arts.

North
Westminster
Community
School

Headteacher: Professor Michael Marland CBE MA

Figure 2   North Westminster School advertisement in the programme of the
English Baroque Choir

■ Budget

A school cannot have a coherent marketing plan without budgetary provision. With the freedom and scope of Local Management, the school is free to determine the amount of the delegated budget which is spent on any aspect of the school's work. A proportion of this will be needed for marketing. Whereas historical funding has been a starting point for the major spending divisions of, for instance, teachers' salaries or energy, a new spending head is required for marketing and public relations. It is very difficult to establish a sensible figure for the first time.

The most sensible way is to price a few items:

- a decent print run of a brochure suitable for your school;
- a two-column by 100 mm advertisement space in the local paper;
- the typography and printing of a double-sided A4 sheet;
- a mailing to a selected group of organisations in the area.

From such a 'job lot' of items a dummy campaign for a year could be crudely costed. Year by year it will be possible to refine this guestimate.

It is easy to overlook the cost of some items, such as postage, and to under-estimate others, such as good quality printing. It is important not to leave out in-house costs. Not only materials but time costs money, and it is dangerously easy to overlook the time it will take, for instance, to stuff envelopes when mailing leaflets.

■ Cross-subsidy

Cross-subsidy is legitimate and well worth careful planning. I mean by this the use of existing activities and publications for marketing purposes. For instance, the print run of an introduction for parents of new pupils or a GCSE option-choice book can be extended to provide additional copies for marketing purposes. This can be sent to local primary schools or be made available for visiting parents. The 'run-on' costs for these extra copies is obviously much cheaper as the 'origination' costs will have been met. It is thus possible to charge the marketing budget only for the extra copies at that run-on cost. On the other hand, you may wish to use the exercise to improve the size and quality of the original publication itself, in which case the marketing budget would pay for part of the origination costs also. Such cross-subsidy can be mutually beneficial if it is clear what is being done and for how much.

■ Sponsorship

Similarly, sponsorship may be sought for certain forms of marketing. Sometimes this will be a straight donation: perhaps a firm giving money for a soccer team's specially printed shirts. At other times, an event or publication may carry the sponsor's message. This is that rare thing: income to the marketing budget.

The larger the print-run and the circulation, the more attractive the project is to the sponsor, and therefore the greater the potential income. For instance, a literary anthology of students' writing is more likely to attract sponsorship if it is circulated beyond the school, and that brings a higher sponsorship income and allows the use of the larger print-run for the school's marketing – as well as pleasing the student authors whose work has been included.

■ Topping-up

Some of the recommendations for marketing in this book are primarily for the benefit of the life of the school: e.g. a good signing system (page 79) and effective displays (page 84). It would be logical and legitimate to regard the entire budget for those items as lying within 'buildings and maintenance' and 'curriculum events', though it would also be reasonable to top those budgets up with marketing funds if required.

■ 'Selling' marketing

In schools which are short of income, there is likely to be resentment from teachers at money being put into marketing, at least until the benefits are felt. This is best met by full information, economy, and the relating of at least part of the marketing enterprise to improving existing activities and publications. A *'How to Use Northway School'* booklet, which is of obvious direct educational use as well as having marketing potential, is likely to be more acceptable to reluctant marketeers.

■ Conclusion

Few schools will be well-placed to devote great energy, funds, or skill to devising a totally comprehensive and coherent marketing plan. Nevertheless, this is the end towards which we need to be working. It is one in which management structure, job description, expertise, and salary levels of all the senior staff should be related to the overall school aims and plan, and this plan must involve a marketing strategy. The style is indeed part of the message, and the plan should reflect the school's wider educational aims – and reinforce them.

3 Creating a corporate identity

With greater competitiveness, diversification, and decentralisation in the education system, a school has to differentiate itself from other schools in ways that will appeal to parents and the local community as a whole.

▶ **'In order to be effective every organisation needs clear a sense of purpose that people within it understand. They also need a strong sense of belonging. Purpose and belonging are the two facts of identity.'**

That is how Wally Olins, chairman of the design consultancy Wolff Olins and a corporate identity expert, defined identity in his book *The Corporate Personality*. Corporate identity is how an organisation – in our case, a school – sees itself, and communicates that sense of identity to itself and the outside world. Call it school spirit, or ethos, or what you will. Today, it is often called corporate identity.

Public schools such as Eton and Harrow have a corporate identity. We have a definite perception of these schools, for better or worse. Their identity has been carefully nurtured. There is every reason why all schools – independent, local authority maintained, and grant maintained – should develop a corporate image, identity, or style. It can offer valuable benefits to those who work in the school and can help others understand and appreciate what the school is all about.

People have two images of a school: that which is filtered through their general perception of the education system as a whole, and that created by how the school presents itself. (Developing a positive identity that influences how people see a particular school can make them see the education system differently as well.)

■ What is corporate identity?

Corporate identity highlights three things:

- who you are;

- what you do;
- how you do it.

According to Wally Olins, corporate identity shows itself in four ways:

- Products: In our case, the 'products' are the achievements of the pupils; the events, activities, and publications of the school; and, to a lesser extent, the staff and governors. They should reflect the standards and values that are set by the school.

- Environment: The school buildings and how they are designed, furnished, and maintained.

- Communications: How the school communicates internally and externally.

- Behaviour: How a school behaves towards its staff, pupils, parents, and the rest of the community.

Identity, of course, is more than a name. In *The Corporate Personality*, Wally Olins explains:

▶ 'From names it's only a small step to signs, secret or otherwise, heraldry, uniforms and all the other trappings of visual identity. The group, whether it's as small and primitive as Richmal Crompton's *William and his Outlaws* or a sophisticated multinational enterprise like IBM, uses all the visual means available to it to reinforce its own identity, and to make this identity clear to all the different groups with which it deals.'

Identity must be visible, tangible and all-embracing. Schools need to be consistent in their attitude, action, and style.

A school needs to assess, and where necessary or possible, change:

- the internal and external appearance of the building;

- the material produced (such as the school brochure, communications with parents, internal staff and pupil documents);

- the school uniform (or accepted mode of dress); (The *Education Act (No 2) 1986* puts the responsibility for uniform policy in the hands of the school governors.)

- the way school events (such as assemblies, open days, concerts, sports days, and so on) are organised;

- how the school communicates with the media;

- the way staff and pupils relate to each other and how they behave outside the school;

- how the school treats visitors in terms of personal contact and the school environment – reception area, corridors, and so on.

A school should discuss what visual aspects of the school it wishes to develop, such as a school logo, colour scheme, and signing systems, and it should make it and its activities readily identifiable both on-site and elsewhere.

Developing a corporate identity takes time, commitment, and a wide-ranging assessment of all aspects of the school. It means change and some outlay in resources. Yet it can pay dividends to the school and forms a crucial plank in marketing the school successfully.

A corporate identity is not something to hide behind. It says to those who are part of the school, and to the media and general public that these are the standards, values, and attitudes the school works to. If the school departs from those standards, it will show. Similarly, an identity which does not reflect the true nature of the school (who it is, what it does, and how it does it) will soon be discredited.

■ House-style and logo

One way of supporting the corporate identity of the school is the designing and consistent use of a 'logo' within the wider context of a 'house-style'.

With the explosion of typographical styles in the last 50 years came the visual idea that a corporate identity (whether of a commercial organisation or a single project) could be characterised by the projection of its name in a particular typeface and format. This became known by the technical term: *logo*. This is a shortened form of 'logotype', meaning a word ('logo') presented in a particular typeface.

Graphic designers search for a form for a tradename that fuses typeface and words to create an always recognisable image. Often the shape, style, and linkage of the letters are designed uniquely for this purpose, and the form of the typeface and its shape rapidly establishes the letters as a recognisable image – thus embodying the idea of the service, organisation, or product in a clearly recognisable form. Figure 3 shows some well-known logos.

Figure 3   Examples of well-known logos

The possibilities are stylistically infinitely variable and, of course, a school would not wish to commission a design which looked as if it were marketing a washing machine. An existing symbol can be incorporated, whether a crest, a motif (like the tree of Crestwood School, Eastleigh), or an abstract form (like the NW of North Westminster School) in Figure 4.

Figure 4   Two school logos

The logo and associated house-style should be commissioned as a whole from a graphic designer. There may, of course, be a suitably skilled graphic designer on the staff, but it is important to realise that logo designing is a specialised skill, not normally one that a school student or even a professional art teacher gains without considerable experience.

The designer should be given a brief, which specifies the overall style and image being sought, the purpose for which it is most likely to be used, (for example, letter headings, compliment slips, banner headings for posters, etc.), and the range of methods of reproduction (e.g. size, colour, signs, and materials).

It is normally best if the logo is designed integrally with the typeface and layout of the associated information: address and names of senior staff, for instance. This, together with the paper chosen, creates the graphic house-style of the school.

This house-style will speak for the school, subtly giving an impression of the character of the school's work and its aspirations. Modernity, clarity, aesthetic sensitivity, and sense of purpose can be conveyed. Secondly, the logo will remind people of the school and its work rapidly when glimpsed in a variety of contexts. Finally, as the house-style should be used for all publications, signs, and products, it will help to create coherence and a sense of community.

■ Conclusion

A corporate identity plan that is well-researched, widely accepted in the school, and employs good design, can combine style and substance – a style that is attractive to the eye and ear and pleasant to work in; a substance that highlights and enhances the aims, values, and integrity of the school. In forming a coherent marketing policy, establishing, expressing, and making use of corporate identity is of great importance.

4 Market research

Establishing the views of those in the school, and their parents and those who might come to the school, not only helps the running of the school but is a necessary part of marketing the school. No promotion of a school and its work is sensible without knowing what people want and what the school is really doing: promotion cannot persuade people to like something which is not what it says it is.

■■■ The purpose of client research

'Market' or 'client' research, whether we use formal or informal means, should attempt to establish parents' (and thus, of course, their children's) perceptions of what they require. This involves asking a number of uncomfortable questions, especially in establishing to what extent parents are satisfied with what they perceive the school is doing. Their wishes have been influenced by many societal pressures which cannot be changed by schools. People's attitudes will not readily change, and the school may need to change to meet them. If it is not willing or able to, the school must make this decision in the light of a full picture of what parents really want.

When we have done no 'market research' we often have closed ears, and then prejudice and our ignorance of the communities we serve tempts us to parodies of what we think people might want. For instance, since the 1986 legislation requiring the publication of examination results, it is a widely-held view that this would lead to parents choosing schools exclusively on raw examination results. Where did we get that idea from? Only fear. Studies have shown the opposite. For instance, a London-wide study of parents' choice of secondary school in 1986, found that parents, when asked about the characteristics of schools required when choosing, 84.7 per cent mentioned 'discipline/children well behaved', 79.2 per cent 'caring/understanding/friendly teachers', compared with 71.2 per cent 'emphasis of good exam results/children "stretched" academically' (ILEA, 1989, p.11).

Where we can find out parental views, it seems at least sensible to get to know them! The same survey, for instance, found that '69 per cent preferred a school which had a uniform'. That does not mean every secondary school should take that as a direct mandate, but it is surely a 'market research' factor worth knowing.

Of course, different parents will, to some extent, have different wishes – and learning and respecting this variety of views is difficult but necessary. Listening schools will find a huge degree of similarity in the wishes of its parents. They may have gained knowledge of these wishes through different routes and possibly arrived at them for different reasons. Furthermore, they will certainly be expressed in a variety of different styles. That is one reason why I try to meet enquiring parents individually. Each family asks questions aimed at similar targets: the comfort of the child, discipline, keeping in touch, the range of subjects, preparation for examinations, higher education. However, one family often feels awkward putting their questions in front of others, and the formulation of the answer has to differ according to the range of reference, the vocabulary, and the style of question.

Despite these similarities, there are also some real differences. These are at the edges of the central core of concerns. Some parents, for instance, have clearer views about the arts experiences that they want for their children; a few want a specific range of languages; others are keen on their son's or daughter's sporting opportunities. Knowledge of these particular interests and requests is obviously valuable for school planning: Do we cater for this need? If not, could we and should we? It may lead to the decision to add a feature to the school, or it may lead to a decision to continue to leave that feature out on the grounds that we cannot do everything and it would be impracticable to encompass it.

■ How to research your 'market'

Most schools appear to have done very little research, or even used the research that has been done by others. Even the informal information of parents' questions, worries, suggestions, and complaints in interviews, letters, phone calls, and enquiries are rarely systematised.

A first, and easy step therefore, is to ask those staff who most listen to parents to contribute to a quick internal questionnaire on parents' views. A sample list of topics is shown opposite, with the kind of questions asked. Such a rapid summary can be written up to produce a brief report: *What are our parents concerned about?*

What Are Our Parents Concerned About?

The following list of concerns has been compiled
from the points made by parents to colleagues who
have met them, in telephone conversations, or in
letters during last term. The list is not
exhaustive and no attempt has been made to
quantify the frequency of the topics. In each
case the general topic is named first, and then a
typical question from one of our parents.

Homework: 'How do we know how much our son should
do?'
Bullying: 'Nobody actually hits him, but two boys
in the class make Mark feel really
uncomfortable.'
Communication: 'We really don't get replies to
the notes we send Sarah's Tutor.'
Syllabus content: 'We could help Shahid so much
more if we knew which topics he would be covering
in the main subjects.'
Aspirations: 'Our daughter keeps getting good
marks and praise, but she doesn't seem to us to
be really stretched or to be working very hard.'
GCSE language courses: 'Why isn't it possible to
choose from a wider selection of languages?'

Some other ideas for eliciting views from parents are:

- Briefly recording the main concerns and interests expressed by parents considering secondary school choice;

- Inviting parents' comments in circulars about other matters;

- Interviewing a sample of parents of recently joined pupils;

- Introducing an old-fashioned 'suggestions' box;

- Inviting an outsider to spend a couple of days observing the school to give his or her impressions of what is best about its work and atmosphere;

- Commissioning a professional consultant (who might well be a parent) to visit the school and write a report.

Table 1
What parents liked about the school

(Percentage table)

	1983 (N=216)	1984 (N=171)	1985 (N=146)
	%	%	%
School organisation	53	29	53
Teachers	51	33	41
Discipline	28	20	25
Good teaching	8	8	13
Extra-curricular activities	11	5	10
Good academic facilities	11	5	10
Uniform	9	5	6
Sport facilities	7	1	1
Other (e.g. close to home)	6	6	3

Table 2
What parents disliked about the school

(Percentage table)

	1983 (N=216)	1984 (N=171)	1985 (N=146)
	%	%	%
Poor teaching	13	18	25
Poor discipline	16	15	24
Aspects of organisation	26	10	10
Poor academic facilities	3	6	8
Intake not balanced (e.g. ability)	4	4	1
Poor sports facilities	4	3	1
Other (e.g. insufficient homework, difficult travel, poor canteen)	13	2	5

(ILEA, 1986, p.7)

More methodical surveys can be carried out to sample the views of parents of pupils at the school, normally by a postal questionnaire, sometimes supplemented by interview. Alternatively, you might survey parents of pupils still in junior schools, though this is technically harder and more expensive, as it can be difficult to get access to a sample of parents whose children are not already in your school. For a secondary school, a collaborative local primary school is usually necessary, and for primary schools, nurseries – though these will not provide a cross-section sample.

■ Comparing results

The results of these surveys should, when possible, be compared firstly with earlier years and also with any comparative data from elsewhere. Indeed, in some cases, the questionnaire should be devised to facilitate this comparison by its question design. In Tables 1 and 2, for instance, are the answers to the question 'What do you like about your child's school?' and the converse, asked over the first three years of secondary school in the Inner London Education Authority in the early eighties, as recorded in *Attitudes to School: a study of the parents of third-year pupils.*

Such a comparison helps you scrutinise your own data: how does it differ from other research, *and why*?

National data is available occasionally: for instance the 1989 DES-commissioned survey of *'Parental Awareness of School Education'* included such facts as, that 24 per cent of parents had been in touch with a school at some time or other about the amount of homework set. Those who received a written report regarded it 'as helpful principally because' the report:

- provided evidence of progress: 55 per cent

- described the child's behaviour: 42 per cent

- gave information on attainment: 34 per cent

- indicated a child's strengths and weaknesses: 16 per cent

The same survey gave levels of parental satisfaction, and it would be helpful to compare one's school with the national figures. Consider, for instance, the parents' views on 'Why school is not meeting "chosen" child's needs' in Table 3 (page 32).

If your school differs from this, you may want to formulate questions and seek answers to explain the differences.

Table 3 Why school is not meeting needs

Base: All respondents who think 'chosen' child's school is not meeting their needs

	Total	'Chosen' child age 5–10 only	11–16 only	Area Type Rural	Small town	Outer city/ large town	Inner city/ large town	Social class A–C1	C 2–E
	(287) %	(165) %	(122) %	(61) %	(74) %	(105) %	(39) No.	(142) %	(142) %
He/she is capable of more than currently doing/not being pushed hard enough/work is too easy/could be doing more difficult things/not being stretched	29	36	20	30	26	31	(11)	34	25
Not getting the help he/she needs in some or all subjects	11	12	10	13	9	11	(4)	8	13
Should be more individual/small-group teaching as opposed to one big class	7	8	6	3	12	8	(2)	7	8
Would benefit from extra tutoring/ individual tutoring would improve performance	5	5	6	5	4	6	(3)	4	6
Mixed abilities in one class/should be streaming/should separate different ability children	4	4	4	3	3	4	(4)	5	4
Needs more mental stimulation/he/she is bored	4	5	7	3	4	5	(1)	6	3

(DES, 1989, p.21)

The findings will not always be comfortable. Marten Shipman, in his essay in *Education for the Inner City*, recommends developing a partnership with parents to increase the working power of the school. However, he warns:

> ▶ **'Parents have strong and sometimes unwelcome views on education. The political action following attempts to reform secondary education in some West German states is a warning. Even more significant may be North American examples where parents have obtained control.'**

Even if the views elicited are unorthodox or difficult or impossible to accept, there may well be something to be gleaned from them and they are certainly worth knowing.

■ How to research the wider 'market'

So far I have spoken about discovering the views and wishes of clients and future clients. There is also, though, the need in some schools to research the number, range, and location of children who might come to the school. In some, especially rural areas, the potential pupils are limited to the natural 'catchment area' of the school. At the other extreme, there are schools which are so well served by public transport that pupils can criss-cross the town or city to the school of their choice. In these situations a school needs to know who the available pupils are.

For instance, a London secondary school was convinced that the low attainment of their pupils at secondary intake reflected the primary 'output' of the area it mainly served. However, a study showed that the pupils from local primary schools who chose that secondary school did *not* represent the full cross-section of local primary children, and most of those with high attainment at transfer opted out of the area to church or voluntary-aided schools.

A small-town country school found out the number and attainment of children opting out of its area to a neighbouring large town, and then established those as a target to persuade them to stay in their home town and use that school.

If a school wishes to expand its intake, its pupils transferring (perhaps to the two-year GCSE course), or the balance of its intake (whether by gender, ethnicity, or attainment), it needs to know the whereabouts of young people who could come to the school.

5 How to communicate in print

Within any coherent marketing plan there will be a very large place for printed material. Many examples are a normal part of the work of the school, but some will be specially devised for marketing. A school should review its existing regular and occasional publications, using this check list, and consider which could be added to its own list.

The range of publications from a school

Calendar
Standard letters
Pupils' writing
Pupils' diaries
Pupils' guides
Parents' guides
Christmas cards
Newsletter
Pupils' records of achievement
Pupils' school reports
Examination results
Posters for events
Publicity leaflet
Brochure/prospectus
Programmes for performances and events
Governors' report to parents

Look at this list with these points in mind:

- How can the school's wider message be better put across by its publications?

- Can some of the routine material (like uniform lists) have a supplementary purpose?

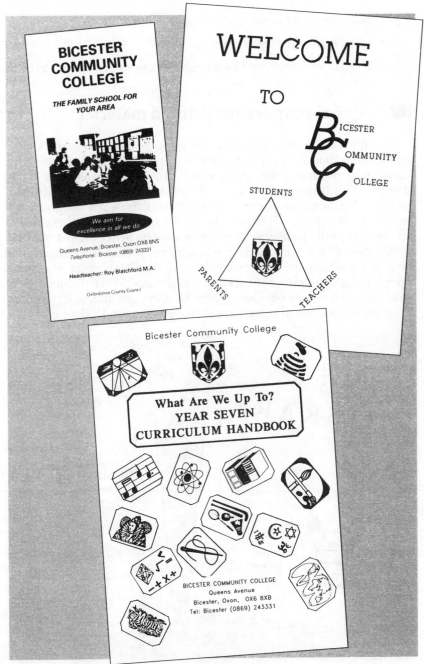

Figure 5   Promoting different aspects of a school

- Is the designed house-style being well applied?
- Is the tone of the text appropriate?
- Is the school portrayed by its publications as you want it to be?

◼ A dual purpose for printed material

Brochures and publicity leaflets may be regarded as pure 'marketing' publications, but there are many forms of publication which serve the curriculum and life of the school which can also serve as a marketing device. This dual purpose gives the promotional aspect additional strength: for the prime purpose of a publication is clearly integral to the needs of the school. This function itself speaks of the work of the school and so the promotional function may be better carried out by a publication which is entirely for publicity purposes. For instance, one task of a promotional brochure will be to detail the range of courses open to older students. This can in some ways be better done by the students' own course booklets, which for some promotional purposes, are more authentic and persuasive than a prospectus. Realia convinces.

Figure 5 (continued)

▪ Copywriting

The printed word will carry the school's voice to more people and in a more permanent form than almost any other aspect of the school's work, and is worth taking great care with, and requires skill.

'Copy' is a noun hardly heard in schools in its meaning: 'material to be printed, e.g. typescripts, photographs, and line drawings.'

Yes, just another word for 'writing', but the use of the word focuses on the purpose of the writing: it is to be set in type according to a designed lay-out and printed in some form of publication whether notice-board, leaflet, or advertisement. In each case the printed version will be read by a number of people, mostly unknown to the writer. Furthermore, in many cases the writer is not writing for himself, but on behalf of the school and its corporate identity. Thus this copy inevitably works to different conventions than, say, letters, essays, or even memoranda.

▪ The copywriter

Often, for writing copy, collaboration between a professional copywriter and a specialist from the school is a practical idea. The copywriter can 'interview' the school specialist and be briefed by her or him. From that, and the perusal of any background documents, a good writer can often make an excellent job, capturing facts, tone, and style in a simple but clear way. It is worth having existing documents read and commented on by such a person too.

The specific style required for a Press Release is outlined on pages 58-61. Are there, though, any general principles that apply to all copy?

▪ Audience

The first point is the need for a sense of audience. It is an axiom of late-twentieth century writing that whatever the content, the author has to have a 'sense of audience'. It is often wise to arrange for the same set of ideas, arguments, or facts to be written up in different ways for different readers. A school needs to have a sharp sense of audience, and to present its points appropriately for each. This means the use of language which is personal, vivid, precise, and brief. The following standard advice about copywriting, in general, would apply to schools.

■ Features and benefits

In both written and oral presentations it is important to be aware of the distinction between features and benefits, and to highlight the benefits which derive from the features. It is tempting to rest one's case on features alone, and schools especially tend to do this: 'Our classes are organised in...'; 'This school's curriculum has...'. Such statements risk the response 'So what?'

Because we are 'convinced' of the strengths of our own organisational pattern or our activities, we too readily assume that naming a feature of the school is automatically to persuade. The writer has to change a mere feature into a *benefit* that attracts the keen parent.

'Five forms of entry' and 'three years in one of the Lower Houses' are features which are not in themselves of any special interest and certainly do not suggest any benefit for *my* child's education. However, the benefits can be brought out: 'The small Lower House, with only 450 pupils and none of them over 15, encourages a calm, hard-working and friendly atmosphere in which every girl and boy can be well-known, comfortable, and able to work happily'. This description brings out benefits rather than mere features.

■ Making copy count

A useful guide to writing good copy is the method abbreviated to the acronym AIDA, now updated to AID(C)A. The letters stand for:

- **Attract** How do you catch the reader's attention and make sure they want to read on?

- **Interest** How do you continue to keep the reader's interest?

- **Desire** How do you arouse the desire of the reader to want to do or to want to have what is offered?

- **Conviction** How do you convince the reader that what you are saying is true?

- **Action** How do you get the reader to take the action you want him or her to take?

The advertising industry call this the 'hierarchy of effects' to explain the stages of how advertisers influence their audiences. You can use it for any form of printing material – from a letter to parents to the school brochure.

■ School publications

Even the most mundane practical publications of the school have a marketing value. For instance, a larger number of schools use a form of diary booklet for pupils, which is both a pupil work-planning device and whole-school liaison device. Although devised for practical internal reasons, a well-thought out diary booklet, well printed and set out, is itself an advertising document, and can be part of a pack of materials presented to visitors.

The historical booklet described on page 51 had as its prime purpose the ceremony of the rededication of the stone from the local alms-house, but was also a history of the school site. On sale subsequently at reception and used as a gift to some visitors, it was clearly also a marketing device, making a strong statement about the intellectual interests of the school.

For some years it has been my habit to extend the print-run of documents like student literary collections, Awards Evening programmes, and invitations to special events, and to use them as marketing documents in their own right. Even the school calendar, if indeed interesting things do take place and if it is well designed, can be a useful marketing handout.

The entire range, despite the expected variety, should have the unity of a visual house-style (see pages 24-26). Within this style there should be a unity in the diversity, so that every example speaks of the tone and style of the school's work. In this context it is very important that the words of the publications maintain this target of quality.

Whatever printed communications the school is putting out, however mundane they may seem, you should try to apply the highest standards of presentation and content of them (see Fig. 6 on page 40).

■ Letters to families

Every school puts out a range of functional letters with dates, occasional closures, and changes of routine. Sadly, these are often rushed off, stating the facts baldly, often awkwardly, and occasionally brusquely. It is rare for them to be used for positive promotion.

It is not cynical to point out that facts can be presented more or less positively, and misleading impressions can easily be given. For instance, every school has to have five days of teacher work, perhaps best thought of as 'professional development days', in addition to the 190 teaching days. In many schools these have to be placed during a term, and some schools place them mid-week. This can look to parents

BICESTER COMMUNITY COLLEGE NEWSLETTER

Dear Parents

A short and very busy Spring Term draws to a close. In addition to all the usual academic work at this time of the year pupils have been involved in a wide range of extra-curricular activities: Maths Roadshows; History & Geography visits to London; Careers Fairs in Birmingham; production of the Voice Over newspaper for Goodhead Press, a Theological Conference and Crime Prevention Quiz; charity fund raising - and lots of sport!

Inspectors' Report on the School

This has also been a term in which we have produced a report for the Local Education Authority and County Councillors on the quality of learning and teaching in the school. The exercise has been a valuable one for the teaching staff and has given us the opportunity to 'take stock' and plan for the future. If any parent would like to talk about the Report, please contact the Headteacher.

One comment from a visiting adviser reinforced our own view about the atmosphere and ethos of Bicester Community College. I quote:

"There appeared to be open communication and a supportive atmosphere within the Community College. Students appeared to be well-ordered and considerate in the corridors with the exception of one bottle-neck near the end of the day.

There appeared to be respect and good relationships between pupils, and between pupils and staff."

Planning for 1991/92

We shall have our remaining 3 In-Service Training Days in the Summer Term:

Monday 8th April - examining GCSE work
Friday 3rd May - National Curriculum assessment, together with all primary/secondary schools in the Bicester District
Monday 1st July - forward-planning for academic departments.

Staff News

Following interviews with governors Mrs Cynthia Bartlett has been appointed as our new Deputy Headteacher. She takes up post immediately after Easter.

Following the resignation of Mr Colin Hughes as a school governor, Mr John Richardson has been co-opted onto the governing body.

Parents and long-standing friends of the school will probably have read of the recent death of Mr Ewart Clothier, headteacher of Bicester Grammar School from January 1941 to September 1963. His family have decided to set up a Trust for Bicester Community College, in his name.

25th Anniversary

In July 1991 the School and Community College are 25 years old. To celebrate the silver anniversary we shall be staging various events in the week beginning 1st July, including reunions for former staff, pupils and parents.

Figure 6 Communicating with parents

as if it is a 'closure' for pupils, who are therefore *losing* a day. Here is
one school's letter home announcing such a day:

```
Dear Parent,
Re: Teachers' In-Service Training Day - 25 October.
May I remind you that the school will be closed
to students on Wednesday, 25th October, 1990.
This will allow teachers to participate in a
special training session...
```

Put like that, there will be a ripple of indignation from many readers
who do not understand that this does not take a day away from
students. The old–fashioned 'Re' adds to the awkwardness of the tone.
'The school will be closed to students' is unnecessarily offensive. The
letter could be phrased in the reverse way!

```
Dear Parents or Guardians,
Wednesday, 25th October, 1990.
As we announced in the Calendar we sent you at
the start of the year, this is not a school day
for pupils.
Of course, the total length of the school year
remains the same wherever we place the school
days.  Your Parents' Association Committee is
considering the best placement for next year.
You may be interested to know that all the staff
will be here next Wednesday, and we shall be
working on further development of the
curriculum.
```

Even genuinely bad news – such as a closure enforced by burst water
mains – can be put across so as to elicit more or less sympathy.

Most routine letters can also be used to carry positive messages
about interesting developments or future events. Including these items
of news can both soften the impact of bad news and further publicise
the event. A school's mailing is a potentially powerful advertising
medium for the image and events of the school.

■ Newsletters

A regular newsletter (under whatever name) lies happily across the divide between necessary publications, adjusted and also used for publicity, and those designed solely for publicity. In a way, its very obvious prime function of keeping the community of the school informed of its own activities strengthens its power as a promotional tool.

In a way the model is the 'house journal' produced by many commercial organisations for their own staff and customers. Such publications keep the constituent parts of a large and diverse organisation in touch, so that different departments, and those with different tasks in an organisation, can learn of each other's work.

Even a small school can benefit from this, but a school newsletter has the immensely added task of keeping parents in touch, those 'distant clients' whose major sources of information without one is the erratically focused news relayed by their children.

The wider circulation of a school newsletter to public libraries, churches, doctors' waiting rooms, and local associations is an additional promotional benefit, as is further distribution to parents of possible new pupils.

■ What will it cost?

Costs of such a newsletter can be defrayed by charging a subscription or asking for voluntary contributions and soliciting advertising. If the exercise is to be properly costed, staff time should be included, as should printing time and paper or any postal costs. Two A4 pages of advertising might cover all these costs, but only if the time to gather those advertisements is also properly costed in – for this can take considerable time and genial persistence.

■ Who will produce it?

As a newsletter has to be regular, it is a considerably more daunting undertaking than a one-off publication, and the question of whether or not to start one, needs extremely careful consideration. For many schools it may be impossible to find the human resources. For others, though, the effort will be very worth the expenditure – by further building up the school's coherence, working relationship with families, and marketing power.

Undoubtedly the best way to produce such a newsletter is not open to most schools: that is to have a professional writer both to research content and to write it up. Both these tasks can be difficult, require skill, and take time. However, some lucky schools have a parent, teacher or governor, who has these skills and is prepared to take on the task. Other schools have a teacher with these skills. Figure 7 is an example of a very successful primary school newsletter, produced largely by the Headteacher, who does most of the writing, editing, and production herself.

Figure 7   A primary school newsletter

Obviously a newsletter must have an 'editor', and she or he must have the time and resources to put the newsletter together. Whether a teacher, another member of staff, or a parent, time is the main requirement. The temptation in a medium or large-sized school is to give a teacher an Incentive Allowance, say an A or a B, but not the time.

The amount of time required will, of course, depend on the frequency and the length of the newsletter. Once a month is probably the most frequent that is worthwhile; more often than that and the publication will not be read properly. For most schools once a half-term is probably sufficient, and for some, once a term will be all that can be managed. A fair estimate is that, for gathering content, interviewing, writing and 'making up' a half-termly publication, the editor will need a day a week. A teacher's salary at the top of the Standard National Scale plus on-costs can be divided by five and an appropriate Incentive Allowance added to give the 'editorial' costs.

■ How will the newsletter be produced?

Although the general points already made about publication design (see pages 24-26) apply, a newsletter, whatever its frequency, has its own typographical conventions and requirements dictated by speed and convenience.

Essentially a banner-head needs to be designed to top the page and carry the bold title and school logo. This must be designed integrally with the column layout used. That in its turn, needs to be flexible enough for variety (so, for example, you can have the occasional picture across two columns), but simple enough to be laid out easily.

Almost certainly the 'typesetting' should be done in school and 'camera-ready copy' produced on a suitable desk-top publishing package. It does not require very great skill or experience to key in the copy to fit a well designed layout. The hardest part is writing straight into a length convenient for the layout or adapting the copy to fit suitable column units. *That* is a technical skill that can be learnt and once learnt will make a newsletter much quicker to produce.

Figure 8 Two secondary school newsletters

■ Statutory information

Most of the recommendations in this book are about how to extend the information given out beyond the norm, in order to increase the 'presence' of the school and its work. However, there is a sense in which the law has got there first: every school is required by statute to publish certain basic information. The trend of legislation in the eighties included a notion with deeper roots, such as the Taylor Report (*A New Partnership for Our Schools*, 1977), that local communities in general, and parents in particular, should have more influence over schools, that parents should have considerably greater choice – and thus that a range of information should statutorily be provided to help them make choices.

The key legislation is Section 20 of the *Education (No. 2) Act 1986*:

> ▶ **'The Secretary of State shall make regulations requiring the governing body of every county, voluntary and maintained special school to make available to parents of registered pupils at the school, in such form and manner and at such times as may be prescribed:**
>
> **(a) such information as to any syllabuses to be followed by those pupils; and**
>
> **(b) such other information as to the educational provision made for them by the school:**
>
> **as may be prescribed.'**

Further, governors have to report to parents every year, and the form of this report is determined by that same Act, Sections 30 and 31. It is worth studying the primary legislation in full; and this together with extracts from the Statutory Instruments (1989 No. 954) derived from it are reprinted in the Appendix on page 105.

The important factor is that parents have a firm legislative *right* to certain information, especially in the form of an annual statement about aspects of the school's curriculum and in the form of the annual report by governors.

Clearly this obligation should be taken up in a positive spirit, and the letter of the law used in the spirit of putting parents in the picture. Such reports can be promotional in the fullest and best sense of the concept if they are not routine, but rather drafted with enthusiasm, well presented, and complemented by additional descriptions. The minimum statutory requirements should not be merely grudgingly met, but should be exploited as a further opportunity to speak for the school.

◼ Brochures and prospectuses

The most likely way of marketing the statutory need for information to families, both considering the school and currently using it for their children, is a descriptive and explanatory booklet, sometimes called a 'brochure' or a prospectus – though neither title is required and it is usually better to devise your own title.

Unfortunately school brochures are one of the biggest failures in the marketing of schools. Too many schools see them only as an annual report or handbook. Too little thought goes into what they should contain, how they should look, and who is going to read them. But the brochure is a key marketing tool for the school and should be considered with great care.

Figure 9   School brochures

■ What should the brochure aim to do?

The school brochure does not have to tell parents and others everything about a school, but can concentrate on the essential elements which that school wishes to put across. It must be succinct, attractive, informative, and relevant to its specific purpose. That purpose is to 'sell' the school, so it must have both style and substance.

A parent wants to know: Is this the sort of school I would send my child to? And the school wants its brochure to make that parent sufficiently interested to get in touch, come and look round, and talk to the staff about the school.

If the brochure is to go to local businesses and industry as well, it must make them sit up and think: this is the sort of school we want our future employees and colleagues to come from; or we want to get involved in supporting this school.

■ Planning the brochure

First work out how large you want, or can afford, the brochure to be, in terms of number of pages and size (A4, A5, and so on). Obtain some estimates from printers to see what the cost is likely to be. (Check the cost of some colour element and for different ways of producing the brochure. Local printers are often happy to advise and help on such matters). Relate how much space you have to play with to what you want to say. This will help you dete.mine how succinct you must be, how much space you have for photographs and illustrations, and what options there are for design. Don't try to cram too much into the space you have available.

Decide what information you want to get across. Divide this into logical sections, such as:

- What do we stand for? – aims and values;

- How are we organised? – academic and administrative structures;

- What can we offer? – curriculum, facilities, activities;

- Who are we? – teaching and administrative staff (possibly just Headteacher), Heads of Departments with photographs, governors, PTA. (A full staff list can be given but is probably not especially valuable).

This list is just a jumping-off point for assessing your own priorities and ideas. The order, the degree of detail, and the style must be personal to the school whilst meeting the statutory requirements.

▄▄ Choosing your words

A very interesting technical point is the relationship of the text of the brochure to the 'original' documents, such as the aims of the school as agreed by the governors to meet Section 23 of the *Education Act 1986*, the formal description of the curriculum, or the examination results. On the one hand, the brochure must be authentic, but on the other hand, the full text in its original form may be necessary for its legal or functional purpose, but not be right for *this* reading. For instance, the formal 'aims' may be too long, detailed, and cautiously worded. All the main text of the brochure might need is edited highlights – the key phrases. Perhaps the full text could be printed in an annex.

Similarly, the correct professional jargon of curriculum planning may not be suitable for this purpose: 'cross-curriculum themes' is not a self-evident, or indeed, entirely logical phrase. The school may wish to devise a public statement that is phrased differently from that used internally. Normally it is best to use plain English and avoid the profession's jargon. If you wish to, some features like key examination results, key staff names, and forthcoming dates can be printed on loose sheets, suitably designed, which are held in an internal back cover pocket.

▄▄ Illustration

Take and select good photographs to illustrate key aspects of the school. Make sure they are as natural as possible rather than looking too posed. Make sure, too, that text and photographs reflect the cultural and ethnic mix of the school and also the equal opportunities that the school is sure to be promoting. If possible, the photographs should give a sample of the range of people and range of activities the school offers – so that activities like parents consulting with teachers are not inadvertently left out.

▄▄ Seeking criticism

Because it is always difficult for an insider to judge a presentation of the school, show the proposed text and photographs to representatives of different groups in the school – and to those at whom you are aiming the brochure, namely parents and business-people outside the school. In short, seek an objective, outsider's view as well as that of those working in the school.

If you have succeeded, the brochure as a whole will be a coherent and balanced publication that reflects the best of the school as a whole.

■ Mailing

Mailing is one of the most closely-targeted methods of communicating about the school. It is worth considering seriously and not just leaving to chance. By preparing and using carefully constructed mailing lists, the school can build up a network of well-informed supporters.

Any comprehensive marketing plan should include mailing. Most commercial organisations have to seek out the people to whom to address mailings and spend considerable sums on building up mailing lists. Schools are better placed: their pupils' families are already the recipients of a range of school letters. They are your ready-made mailing list, which can legitimately be used for a variety of promotional purposes.

The LEA's primary schools are also on a ready-made list, reached through an LEA circulation or by direct posting. The primary schools are, of course, channels to the parents of their pupils, their governors, and their teachers. A number of occasions may arise for sending information, invitations, and school publications to any of those groups – including the pupils themselves.

In addition, though, other mailing lists should be drawn up including certain kinds of firms, voluntary organisations, places of worship, higher education, and certain professional groups.

■ Storing mailing lists

The best way to store lists is to use a suitable computer data-base programme to keep an up-to-date list of names and addresses which can be altered easily and regularly. It is important to stress that this list *must be kept up-to-date* or it soon becomes useless and merely shows that the school does not really care about its audience. You know yourself how irritating it is to be sent information from an organisation with which you are no longer connected.

The names on your programme can be coded into certain 'fields' by type. Adhesive labels can then be printed by classification as required. It is helpful to have at least one set printed and put on to envelopes, which can be at the ready for the next dispatch. These can then be prepared in less busy moments, and the decision to send out a mailing is not held up by the time-consuming envelope addressing – or even stamping, as they can be waiting pre-franked.

■ Conclusion

In a way, any school is a mini-publishing house, with the printed word essential to many of its pedagogic and communicative tasks. Many of these can be adapted, not only to have a marketing function, but also to gain from the adjustment. Others will originate as marketing exercises, but will be found other uses.

Some of these can be additionally funded by external sponsors. It is worth noting that, as with all sponsorship, it can be difficult to know who is gaining most from this – the sponsor or the school. What may look like an advertisement endeavouring to gain goodwill for the sponsor is also frequently a way in which the approbation of the sponsor is credited to the school. Thus, a booklet of the history of one of the North Westminster School sites, sponsored by a major property development company, reminds readers that such a major company thinks it worthwhile to invest in the work of this school. Similarly, booklets of older students' short stories published at North Westminster, gives the students additional satisfaction when their work is sponsored by a major firm.

Such sponsorships become easier to seek when you have two or three examples to show, in which good design and printing support the work of students, or an interesting picture of the life of the school. Once a sponsor has filled a back cover or inside front cover, it is attractive to others to do likewise.

There is a world of difference between the school that proffers meanly typed basic circulars and one that uses type, illustration, design, text, and overall format in a range of publications to speak to the school and speak for the school.

6 Advertising

Generally speaking, every activity described in this book is a form of advertising. Within that, though, there is also the specific skill of designing, writing, and placing of advertisements in paid positions.

Some people consider that advertising is an essential part of promoting a school; others sound a note of caution, seeing it as both an expensive and a highly professional activity in which schools must work hard to compete well.

Advertising is not, in itself, immoral or wrong. So long as it is 'legal, decent, honest and truthful', the only thing you can do wrong is to run an unsuccessful advert.

■ What to advertise

You want to advertise the school and its advantages. The starting point for developing your advertising strategy can come out of your SWOT assessment of the school. This acronym stands for Strengths, Weaknesses, Opportunities, Threats (see page 10). You may decide to highlight the strengths or draw attention away from the weaknesses while they are being dealt with. You can identify opportunities for running adverts on the school in relation to specific events – good exam results, the opening of new buildings, winning a national award. You may also need to respond positively to certain threats to the school, such as proposed closure or amalgamation, uninformed attacks on education by public figures locally or nationally, local schools seeking to attract a dwindling pool of potential pupils.

Above all, you need a 'unique selling point'. What is different or special about your school? Is it the ethos or tradition, the environment, the exam success, the facilities?

You may want to draw several selling points together in a long-term advertising plan with specific times of increased advertising activity. If your main purpose is to attract pupils to the school, then you need to make parents aware of your school and its advantages well before the official period of choosing a school.

When you are planning your advertising you should avoid:

- making comparisons between your school and other schools;

- not taking account of the culture, lifestyle, ethnicity, and religions of the people you want to reach;

- offering confusing or too many messages. (Keep it simple: one ad, one message.)

Where to advertise

Once you have decided that you need to advertise you must decide how best to reach your intended audience, and how much information you want to give them. Outlets for advertising include local and national newspapers and magazines, educational guides, poster sites, local commercial radio, leaflets, brochures, direct mailing, exhibitions and stands.

When you are considering an advertisement you need to decide:

- What message you want to get across;

- The target-audience you want to reach: for example, is it the whole local community, all the parents (or just those who are deciding to which secondary school to send their child), or prospective teachers?

- How much you want, or have available, to spend;

- What media to use;

- How to assess the success of your advertising.

Anywhere there are posters now, there you can advertise too. Just identify the places your audience frequents or passes by – the railway or bus station, supermarket, banks, sports or arts centre.

Find out what they read. Check the circulation of local papers (paid-for and free sheets) and any market research they may have done. If you are targeting a specific geographical area, check which papers sell best there.

Planning a campaign

A general-awareness campaign may require posters in prominent public places and adverts in the local press and on local radio. A more sophisticated campaign intended to get across an argument, set out an issue, or explain school policy or organisation, may require leaflets or brochures or a more carefully devised poster. Remember, the more text or copy on a poster, the better designed (or eye-catching) it has to be to attract and hold interest.

Plan your campaign well in advance. Check the time needed by different media for booking an advert.

Decide where you want the advert(s) to go. You pay more for a prominent position in a magazine or newspaper. Confirm the arrangements in writing with the advertising department. If they make a mistake, you can get your money back or have the advert run again for free.

■ What should go in an advert?

- Do not cram too much into an advert – match the words to the space available.

- If you want people to respond to you, don't forget to add your address and/or phone number.

- Include a small identification mark so you know which adverts people are responding to. For example, ask people to quote a reference number or letter when replying, or ask people where they read or heard an advert about the school.

- Always check for spelling or typesetting errors before okaying an advert for publication. It's no good having an advert about high standards which has a spelling error. Even the most careful organisations can slip up in this way.

■ What will it cost?

Advertising can be expensive. You need to make every pound count, and relate what you spend to your own resources, to what school governors and staff consider acceptable, and to the success rate of your advertising (lack of success may mean upping spending; a good return may enable you to reduce future spending).

Work out:

copywriting and editing costs;

photography costs;

design costs;

printing or recording costs.

- Get the best deal you can from those selling advertising space – ask about special offers for a series of adverts if this is really appropriate.

- Consider offering a poster-site agency a site on the school grounds, with an arrangement to allow you to advertise the school on the site at specific key times of the year.

- Try to obtain backing from sponsors who might fund all or part of the costs of an advertising campaign, or offer space for an advert or an exhibition stand at a reduced rate. (Chapter 12 on Sponsorship will tell you more about the pitfalls and benefits of this.)

- Organise two types of campaign to run together: one using cheap advertising space such as local listings magazines or columns and small ads; the other using more expensive advertising opportunities, such as display ads, posters, and so on.

- Maximise the value of your advertising campaign by setting up interviews on local radio or television, or articles in the press at the same time as you are running the campaign.

7 In the news

The press and broadcasting offer enormous opportunities to highlight the positive side of your own school and of schools generally. They can also pose difficulties and create embarrassment when they find out that something has gone wrong. Here are two sides of the same coin – and a school must be prepared for both. Being seen to handle a problem with confidence and authority can bring as many benefits to a school as publicity for success.

■ Opportunities and dangers

Heads and teachers are justifiably angry when the media make sweeping generalisations about the state of schools, the quality of staff, or the level of standards. It is, therefore, wise not to generalise in turn about the media. To do so merely limits your ability to assess and draw on the benefits and to cope with the difficulties.

Editors and journalists are not 'out to get schools' – although it does happen. What they *do* want is 'a good story' – and that means good news just as much as bad news. Sometimes, it is not so clear cut. For example, running stories on teacher shortages or lack of resources highlights inadequacies in schools, but the publicity can put pressure on local authorities or central government to do something to ease the problems.

If something does go wrong, a journalist has every right to find out the details. Schools are public agencies providing an essential service to society which is financed, largely, by taxpayers' money. How a story comes across in print, on radio or TV depends partly on how the school responds to those enquiries, partly on the quality of the journalist, and partly on the editorial process the story goes through.

Schools appear in the media in three main ways:

- The Headteacher, chair of the governors, or a teacher may be an expert on an educational issue or a 'talking head', which the media uses regularly to comment on education. The school is not directly involved, but may receive some local benefit from this – depending on whether people agree with what the 'talking head' says.

- The school may be used as an example to highlight an educational issue for a newspaper or magazine article, a radio or TV programme, or a news broadcast. Here the school would have agreed to be involved.

- The school is the subject of a news story. This may be with or without its involvement.

Schools need to take the initiative in working with the media by:

- making and maintaining contacts;

- writing press releases;

- understanding how the media works;

- matching their agenda (good coverage) with the media's agenda (a good story).

Making contacts

Keep a checklist of people in the media who will be interested in education stories:

Press

- Education correspondents and writers for the national press – newspapers and magazines.

- News editors of regional and local press – try to identify specific reporters who cover education stories.

Broadcasting

- News editors of relevant television stations – BBC and ITV regional stations.

- News editors and reporters at local radio stations.

Agencies

- Local and regional news agencies and the national Press Association which passes stories on to all national and local newspapers, radio and TV stations.

- Identify newspaper and magazine sections, radio and television programmes which may be useful – and check who edits them.

Your business may be education, but your constituency is the whole of life! As a school, you will deal with issues about health, the arts, sport, design, business, equal opportunities, and so on. So you can gain coverage in sections or programmes other than those dealing specifically with education – for example, health, arts and women's sections or programmes; chat shows and sports programmes.

- Invite media people to school events; offer them a special briefing about the school; send them regular information about events, developments, achievements; ask them to come and talk to pupils about their work.

- Don't overwhelm contacts with stories about the school – and don't pester them about covering the school. Avoid the media response – 'not *that* school again'. Pace yourself – offer good stories at regular, but not too regular, intervals. There is no hard and fast rule, because the unexpected always happens. But aim to offer up to three good stories a term. You will gain credibility – and coverage – by supplying newsworthy or photogenic material.

- Time some stories to key dates for the media. For example, they like to run education stories at the beginning of school terms and for nationwide happenings such as the exam season.

- Even if you use a public relations consultant, make sure you continue to maintain direct contact with the media.

Making and maintaining contacts with the media enables editors and journalists to get to know the school and to set incidents, developments, events – good and bad, in the context of what they already know about the school. They can also make comparisons between schools in your area. This, of course, can be double-edged – they may know that an 'innovative' scheme at your school isn't so innovative because two other schools are running similar schemes. But they will also know when your school is standing out from the rest.

These contacts also encourage a two-way traffic – the media will come to you to report as an example of some educational development.

▪ Writing press releases

A press release is a device which lets a lot of editors and journalists know about an event at the same time. It puts the essential information right into their hands. A good press release is often reprinted virtually verbatim. (This might also be due to a lazy journalist or sub-editor.) But if your press release isn't immediately interesting, you are wasting your time. Most end up in the bin.

▇ Why write a press release?

- You want publicity – for an event about to happen or to report something that has happened, for setting out the views of the school, for setting the record straight in a controversy.
- It is effective in terms of time, effort and money.
- It helps journalists get the facts right.
- It shows you mean business.

A press release must be succinct, accurate, and interesting. You need to say what is happening (or has happened), to whom, when, where, how and why. You must decide why the event is worth publicising and what you want to say about it.

Timing is very important. For example, you need to know when different papers, magazines, radio and TV programmes finalise their contents or 'go to press'. The more dramatic the event, the closer to the deadline you can go.

If you want to publicise a forthcoming school event, then send a short, preliminary press release about three weeks before the event, stating what the event is, and when and where it is happening.

Highlight the newsworthy aspect of the event. For example, if someone famous is to present prizes or open a new building, say who it is. And the more newsworthy, the more you highlight the name. (Look at newspaper billboards – when it says 'Famous film star dies' it means he wasn't all that famous otherwise the name would have been mentioned.)

So your headline should be:

IAN BOTHAM TO OPEN NEW SPORTS HALL

and not:

WELL-KNOWN SPORTSMAN
TO ATTEND SCHOOL EVENT

A week before the event, send a follow-up release with the full details.

◼ What to say

Get the important point across in the first paragraph of the press release. For example:

> Pupils at Michelangelo comprehensive have gained a record number of GCSE passes this year. Not one pupil failed an exam – and 90% scored a top grade A.

> 'We will fight the closure of our school right up to the House of Lords,' said Mary Shelley, chair of the governors at Elisabeth Frink high school.

> Seven-year-old Aziz Kami, a pupil at Henri Rousseau primary school, has been chosen for the county chess team in the national championships next month.

Journalists want basic, relevant and accurate facts fast. Check your facts and the spelling of names. Give people's first name and surname – not initials; and state their age whenever appropriate.

If you want to give some background on an issue, put this at the end of the release under 'Notes to Editors'. This enables you to keep the main body of the release short and snappy.

It is sometimes worth sending different press releases to different sections of the media. For example, one tailored for the local media and one for the specialist education press, which would need more background.

Always give names, phone numbers (work and home) and job titles of people who can give journalists more information. Make sure they know that the media will be contacting them – and alert the school office that there will be calls about the press release.

Check that the person who knows most about the issue being publicised is not going to be away while you are trying to interest the media in the story.

If the story is about named pupils' achievement, check with the parents that they want the media to talk to their children

▬ The mechanics of a press release

- It is worth having special press-release sheets designed. These should reflect the house-style of the school, but you might ask pupils to submit designs within this context.

- Type double – or one-and-a-half – spaced, with wide margins left and right (at least 30mm).

- If the release runs to more than one page, type 'more follows' at the bottom of each sheet. Type 'End' at the end!

- Decide when you want the story to be available for use. If it can be used at any time, type 'FOR IMMEDIATE RELEASE' at the top of the sheet. Always date the release for the day you send it out.

- If it is to be embargoed until a specific time – for example, after a speech, awards ceremony, and so on – type 'EMBARGOED UNTIL 7pm Friday 26 April'. If you are publishing a report, magazine or book of the school, it is better to embargo it so that the media carry the story at the same time.

- Decide on a headline.

- Write the release; check for typing errors.

- Add any 'notes to editors' and contacts for further information.

- If photographs are available, say so – or enclose one with the release to those most likely to print them.

- If you are launching a publication, such as a school brochure or report, send a copy with the release. (Don't be surprised if a journalist phones and asks for another copy – newsrooms tend to be black holes down which printed material disappears without trace.)

For examples of two different press releases, see Figure 10 on pages 62 and 63.

▬ Dealing with the response

When a journalist phones up about your press release, make sure people at your end know what she or he is referring to.

Make sure that whoever answers the school phone knows to which member(s) of staff to refer journalists. If the relevant staff member is unavailable, find out the journalist's deadline and arrange for the

North
Westminster
Community
School

NEWS

ilea

Penfold Street, London, NW1 6RX
Telephone 01-723 0073

Headmaster: Michael Marland CBE MA
Honorary Professor of Education

embargoed until 7pm Tuesday 27 February

CALL FOR NEW PARTNERSHIP BETWEEN PARENTS AND SCHOOLS

o   A signed understanding of mutual support between parents
    and schools.

o   Parent governors actively representing parents.

o   An emphasis on parental obligations.

o   Class meetings for parents and their children's
    teachers.

Parents and schools should do a formal deal together to
ensure that they both work for the benefit of the pupils,
said Alastair Macbeth at tonight's IBM/North Westminster
Annual Education Lecture in London.

The deal - what Alastair Macbeth calls 'a signed
understanding' - would not be a binding contract, rather a
statement of understanding reflecting the mutually dependent
roles of parents and schools. In the deal, parents would not
only acknowledge that they are legally responsible for their
child's education, but agree to give active support to their
child's learning both at school and at home. The school for
its part would undertake to provide a professional service
backed by a minimum programme of parent-teacher liaison.

/more

Figure 10   Two press releases

North Westminster Community School **NEWS**

Penfold Street. London. NW1 6RX
Telephone 01-723 0073

Headmaster: Michael Marland CBE MA
Honorary Professor of Education

ilea

for immediate release

THE MAN WITH THIRTEEN TONGUES

North Westminster teacher aims for Europe's Polyglot title

North Westminster schoolteacher Alan Bradley heard today that he is in the final of the Polyglot of Europe competition. Next week he flies to Brussels for a verbal grilling in the final on Thursday 17 May against 19 other finalists from all over the continent.

A polyglot is someone who speaks several languages, and the competition, sponsored by the European Commission, is open to anyone who can speak nine or more. Alan speaks 13! The idea is to encourage good communications across Europe - which shouldn't be a problem to Alan with Arabic, Bengali, Danish, English, French, German, Italian, Malay, Portuguese, Russian, Spanish, Turkish, and Urdu all on the tip of his tongue.

Alan (38) teaches English as a second language at the North Westminster Community School. In the early rounds of the competition, he was interviewed over the phone in seven languages by native speakers. In the final he will have to hold conversations in as many languages as possible. Doesn't he get confused? No, says Alan. So what's the secret? Confidence, he adds.

for more information, contact

Alan Bradley at
North Westminster on 262 8000
or at home on 542 1730.

North Westminster headteacher
Michael Marland on 262 8000
or at home on 226 0648.

Tuesday 8 May 1990

Headteacher or another senior staff member to phone back before that time. Stories can be dropped if there is no return call.

Don't be put off if the journalist asks lots of additional and searching questions; don't get cross if she or he asks something that is already in the press release.

Phone up the news editor of those publications or programmes which have not responded, refer to your release, and ask if they have all the information they need for a story. Don't be offended if you find little enthusiasm for, or awareness of, your release. Explain briefly what the release is about, and offer to send another one. You may be pleasantly surprised that an item has already been written or that a reporter is listed to attend your event. Or your call may revive or spark interest. Whatever you do, don't demand to know why they are not running your story!

Don't be despondent if your story is cut back or not used at all, even after you have been told it is being used. A good story can lose out to pressures of too many good stories on one day, or to an issue that just happens to be more newsworthy on that day.

Try to avoid days when it is clear there will be major coverage of other stories locally or nationally, such as council elections or Budget Day. It obviously reduces the space available for other stories.

■ Inside the newsroom

We are in the newsroom at Blueskies Television – or it could be the Daily Browse or the Rutland Gazette. The day opens with an editorial conference which discusses and finalises the stories for that day. Stories for future days may also be discussed, or there will be a separate meeting for this. A new programme may well have a news editor dealing with 'today' and another editor dealing with 'forward planning'.

Researchers and reporters will already be checking facts, interviewing people on the phone, digging around stories and making sure they 'stand up' (is it really news?), setting up face-to-face interviews.

News will be 'breaking' all the time: Press Association material will be coming into the newsroom 'down the wire' via computer or tape; freelance journalists or 'stringers' will be calling in with possible stories; organisations will be trying to drum up interest in stories about themselves; press releases will be coming in by post and fax machine.

People on the newsdesk will be sifting through all this, plus the daily newspapers, to find good stories. They will want a spread of different types of story or news. Reporters will be sent out to cover stories as they break or to do interviews for stories with a longer 'lead-time' – that is, feature-type or embargoed stories which will be printed or broadcast later in the week.

A mid-morning or early-afternoon editorial conference will assess the stories underway. Some will be dropped; new ones will be taken on. A big story may be downgraded to a small one, demanding less space or time. A potentially interesting story fails to deliver (the chairman of a large property company has decided to come in from the ledge high above Canary Wharf); a low-key story may suddenly erupt (a small, peaceful demonstration outside a foreign embassy has turned violent and disrupted rush-hour traffic; police reinforcements are being sent in with riot gear). The result of a court case will not now be announced until the next day: is the story held over or rewritten?

Another story breaks, but all the reporters are out. A decision is made to pull a reporter off one story and on to the new, and at this stage, more interesting story (it may be yours). Life is becoming frantic as the news editor tries to deploy the newsroom's resources to best effect both inside and outside. Someone coming into the newsroom to be interviewed is stuck in the traffic. For another story, a researcher is trying to persuade a reluctant official to be interviewed – the story would be too weak if she refuses. Another interviewee can only be seen between 3 and 3.30 pm and there is no reporter available (anyone of these people could be you).

Gradually, reporters return to write up the story or phone a report in to a sub-editor. The sub-editors go to work on the reporters' stories – checking they make sense and can be understood by an audience or readership coming new to the story, making them more succinct, cutting out any 'padding' or unnecessary words or phrases. Reporter, sub-editor and news editor argue over the accuracy of one sentence: has the subbing changed the meaning? The comments from one of the people interviewed have been dropped completely because the story over-runs. A story that started from a press release may bear little relation to the content and tone of that release. 'Your ' story has become 'their' story.

As the deadline for the programme draws closer, decisions are still being made about the content. One story may win out over another because there is a good photograph to go with it or lively interviews with those involved have been taped or filmed. Even when the programme is on the air, a story may be dropped.

This, in brief and in general, is how newsrooms work in radio and TV stations and in newspaper offices. And this is where you and your story have to make an impact.

■ Getting into print and on the air

News is something that either happens to you – such as the school burning down or a serious accident to a pupil – or which you can create yourself. Outstanding exams success is news – but only if you tell people about it. So you have to be prepared both to react to events and to initiate.

A key question to ask is: is your story news or features? A story about the school burning down, a teachers' strike, or exams success is news. One about an innovative scheme to help talented children is a feature. Both may appear on a news page or programme – the difference to emphasise here is that news stories have a 'sell by' date after which they are stale. A feature can be run at any time unless you provide a time-related 'hook' or 'peg' for the story, such as a visit by American educationalists to see the scheme in operation.

It also means you must decide whom to approach on a paper or programme: the news editor or features editor. (If you do approach the 'wrong' person, newspapers and magazines tend to pass ideas on to more relevant sections; less of this happens at radio and television stations because programmes tend to be more self-contained and even competitive.)

The press release is one way to win media space. Others include:

- writing letters to the press,
- offering ideas to editors, and
- submitting articles yourself.

You will have a better chance of a positive result if the ideas relate to current educational developments. The editor may not print your submitted article but may be interested enough to send a reporter to write a piece instead.

■ Whose agenda?

Your agenda is to get favourable coverage for the school; the media's is different. They want to inform and entertain. They want interest, topicality, and controversy. They also want to tell their readers, listeners, or viewers about happenings that some people don't want publicised. (You may sometimes be on the receiving end of this particular interest.)

Each paper, magazine, radio and TV programme wants people to read or watch it rather than the opposition, to be first to break a new story, to cover a story better than its rivals.

But as well as being different, they also want to be the same. You will find papers, magazines and programmes picking stories up from each other. If a story about the school is run in one paper or on the radio, others may take it up. If this happens, try to offer a different angle or new information on the same story so as to maintain interest.

And then they want to be the same *and* different – running education stories at the same time of year (start of term, when exams are on, when teacher resignation dates come along) but seeking a different or unusual angle.

It is worth taking time to feed these various media desires. To do this you can:

- *Offer one paper or programme an exclusive.* It has to be good – and you run the risk of it being ignored by the rest of the media for favouring one source. But if it is really good, then the rest of the media cannot afford to ignore the story.

- *Put an embargo on a story.* Here you run the risk of someone breaking the embargo. If that happens, first ask yourself: does it matter? If no-one else touches the story, then complain strongly to the embargo-breaking paper or programme. If it does not affect coverage unduly, then merely register your annoyance about the embargo-breaker to other reporters who contact you about the story.

Managing the news

Both you and the media are in the business of 'managing' news. This is less innocent than it sounds. It is all about making sure a story is in the media at the most advantageous time. You want to choose a time which heightens the impact of a favourable story or lessens that of an unfavourable one. A publication wishes to do the same on behalf of its own ideas, principles, or interests.

For example, a school may want good coverage during the period when all schools are trying to recruit staff for the new school year or to persuade parents to send their children to your school. A newspaper may be more interested in whether the schools' recruitment drives are a success or in the schools which are popular or unpopular with parents. A story that is seen merely as 'propaganda' for one school – which you may quite legitimately see as a good marketing ploy – would (or at least, should) get short shrift.

All this is 'fair game', but a paper or programme can react badly if it feels it is being used, or bounced into running a story. If there is a clash of agendas, embargoes get broken or stories abandoned. It's a risk you may feel worth taking.

■ Talking with the media

You will be talking to the media by phone or face to face:

- when the school has sent out a press release and the media responds to it (see below);

- when the media either has a story about the school or wants to use the school and its staff as a source of information about an educational issue. (See below and also the next chapter, **Coping with a crisis**, page 72-76).

Most encounters with the media should be pleasant, and occasionally they will be exhilarating. They are opportunities to put your school and profession across to the world in a positive, confident, and interesting way whether you are promoting a success story or dealing with a controversy. Here are some general points to help you understand and cope with journalists and newsrooms.

- In the newsroom, a story may be passed from one person to another. For example, your first contact may be a researcher who checks out the story, works on background, finds people to interview, and so on. He or she then passes the story on to a reporter or even another researcher working a different shift. The media use permanent staff and freelance staff, full-time and part-time, working daily, weekly or fortnightly shift systems. So you may have to talk to more than one person and go over some of the same ground of a story again.

- Don't assume the researcher or reporter you talk with has a specialist knowledge of schools or the education system generally. Be helpful and informative, not patronising or dismissive. A reporter may not know much about your world, but she or he will know how to get information and comments out of you which you may not wish to divulge.

- Try not to waffle or spout a 'party' line. Reporters tend to have 'put down their pens' because they have heard it all before; it is boring; and it reduces your credibility. You are rooting for your school, not a union, political party or educational philosophy – radical or traditional. Pursue such issues or enthusiasms at other times or only when they are central to the story.

- Don't abuse the reporter or treat her or him as your enemy just because she or he is asking questions. They are trying to get both sides of the story and part of that is putting each side's arguments to the other.

- Be polite, firm, and sound or appear confident. Be open about what you do not know about a situation. Showing aggression or indifference is usually counter-productive – even if the reporter gets aggressive. Stay cool and hold your ground.

- Do not be hoodwinked into confirming or acknowledging facts that are wrong or opinions that you do not hold. You may be asked the same question twice during a conversation, albeit in a different way.

- You have various options in terms of the basis on which you talk to a reporter. Talking 'off the record' means different things to different people. Saying something is 'off the record' is no guarantee it will not appear in print. If you do not want a reporter to report something, do not say it. If you want something to be reported, but do not want to be identified as the source, make that explicit and get the reporter to say that she or he won't identify you.

If you want time to think about how to answer some of the questions, say you will phone back – and do so.

'How much do you know?' seems a fairly harmless question – unless you are coping with a controversial situation. Then a question asked to save going over ground already covered begins to sound like a very defensive one. You may well find yourself playing a cat-and-mouse game where you try to check out what the reporter knows and the reporter tries to extract new facts from you.

■ Being interviewed

When you are invited to be interviewed on radio or television, ask about the context (what is the issue? why ask me?); the format of the programme (news or magazine programme? live or recorded? studio-based or recorded at the school?).

Decide what you want to say and the points you want to make. You must be succinct and will have time to make only two or three points. You can discuss in advance with the interviewer what questions she or he will ask you. Don't be put off by unexpected questions during the interview.

If the interview is recorded, it will not all be used. This has two consequences. You don't have to worry about 'drying' or getting into a tangle with what you are saying – just ask for the question again. The tape will then be edited. Second, only key points from the interview will be used. You may be interviewed for three minutes and find that only 15 seconds is used on the programme. Most news items last between one and three minutes, so the reporter has to tell the story as succinctly as possible. The item will often have to be put together by drawing on and editing interviews from several people.

■ When the story appears

The story will probably not turn out the way you want or expect. You may not be quoted in full. There may not be as much detail as you would like. Tone and style may not meet with your approval. Don't take such a negative attitude! Your story has won out over many other stories. People are being told about your school.

■ Setting the record straight

If a newspaper or magazine article contains a mistake or omits what you consider to be important information, you can write a letter to the editor for publication. On radio and television, there is no opportunity for setting the record straight in the same way. Do not nitpick about minor points. Much that goes out on the media is ephemeral. People remember the general rather than the particular. A mistake or missing detail is usually only important to you.

On the other hand, the letters column can be a useful way to continue a lively public debate about a significant issue.

■ Complaining

If a serious mistake or misrepresentation of a situation has been made, which may have major consequences for the school, contact the editor of the publication or programme concerned. The first thing to sort out is: how did the problem arise? Were you unintentionally misleading, did the reporter get something wrong, was there a misunderstanding as the story went through the production process?

From time to time, a publication or programme will set out to fit the facts to the story it wants to print. If you fall victim to this, complain to the editor.

Decide what you want in return: a printed retraction, a personal letter of apology from the editor, an informal acknowledgement that the paper got it wrong, or merely the registering of the complaint. This depends on how serious the mistake or misrepresentation was. Decide too how useful it will be in the future to have your stories covered in the publication or programme concerned. It is a balance between extracting your pound of flesh, showing you cannot be taken for suckers, and remaining on good terms with the media.

If you are not satisfied with the editor's response, you can take your complaint to one of the media watchdog bodies listed on page 115.

8 Coping with a crisis

There must one day be something which goes wrong: an accident, a pupil fight, a teacher's mistake, even a serious tragedy. The underlying assumption of this book is that the school will project its qualities and achievements. How does this approach relate to difficulties, deficiencies, and things that are indefensible? There is even a possibility that the more successful a school is in raising its profile, the more unwelcome an interest the press will take in any problems! There is nothing local newspaper readers like more than a 'Sink school in trouble again story' except for a 'Top school falls from grace' one! So public relations success can lead to a keener and more gleeful interest by the press if difficulties strike.

On the other hand, a school which has a good reputation with its communities and parents is more readily excused when it makes a mistake. Furthermore, if you have a good working relationship with journalists, they are more likely to come to the problem with both a helpful and fairly generous attitude to you in your time of difficulty, and a view of the school's work that is more likely to be evenhanded or to put the unhappy event in a favourable light.

This raises the possibility of a 'pre-emptive strike': should the school make a statement unpressed by enquiries. If you have a good relationship with certain reporters, and you have helped them in the past, you could consider contacting them, inviting them round, or giving an oral statement. However, a journalist's first loyalty is to her or his employer. If there is a 'good' story there (bad to you), she has to report it straight. The best you can hope for is 'damage limitation'.

■ A press conference

For a major event, you could call a press conference, inviting the national and education press as well as the local and regional ones. The advantages of speaking out first are:

- You can show the school's understanding, competence, and control. The impact of the first hearing of the news on the reporters is controlled by the approach of the school, which can put it in the most favourable light.

- Positive use can be made of the action being taken by the school; the efforts made by the students or staff in the face of the difficulty, or any success which was part of the overall difficulty.

Arrange to have copies of a brief press statement ready for distribution (by hand or fax), using the style and layout recommended in the last chapter. A well written statement may be quoted almost verbatim, if only in extract.

There *are* risks in such a positive approach to a crisis. Journalists, being naturally suspicious, will wonder what the school is trying to cover up – despite being open about the incident in question. Do not assume you will be able to control the press conference; there are sure to be awkward and unexpected questions asked. So be sure of your ground. Do you have all the facts and are you aware of all the implications of the incident or problem? (You will invariably miss something – so have someone there who can think on their feet.)

Do not assume that because the press conference – or a phonecall with a journalist – goes off smoothly that the journalist is not digging elsewhere. You have control within your school but not in LEA offices or with governors or parents who may be phoned up and put off their guard by seemingly innocuous questions from a journalist.

■ Choosing silence

You will not always consider it wise, and it will not always be possible, to attempt a pre-emptive announcement. Sometimes you may realistically hope that bad news may not reach the newspapers, and on other occasions you will have a statement ready but prefer silence (which is not the same as 'no comment'!). For instance, once I reached school on a Monday morning to be handed a notorious Sunday newspaper by the caretaker, which had a heading on an inside spread: 'Sir's a witch'. A part-time teacher had taken part in ritual celebrations of ancient druidic witchcraft and was accused of sleeping with pairs of naked girls. I decided that no statement would be best, but I had a statement ready if asked. My colleague, who was Head of the other school in which the man worked, took action and prompted the local paper in that area to carry the striking headline: 'Head sacks witch'. No doubt readers favoured that action, but it associated that school with the questionable actions, whereas my silence kept my school's name out of the story.

Conversely, a reporter for another Sunday paper arrived unheralded at the school, demanding to see 'The Head'. The reporter declared that I had 'sacked' a builder working on site for 'making love with a girl pupil in a workman's hut in the playground'! My Deputy, rightly judging that on this occasion it was indeed 'The Head' who was needed, sent for me insistently and urgently. On arrival, I simulated ignorance of the reason for the visit and presumed it was a general educational enquiry. I asked how I could help. Then I was able to laughingly deny that it could possibly be true as the school did not *employ* contractors. He dropped the enquiry. Later I discovered that there was a glimmer of truth: a young man working for builders had been sacked (by the builder, of course) and a girl had been in a hut!

There are certainly some occasions when it is wisest not to advertise the difficulty and even to be reticent to enquiries. However, tactics of suppression and evasion should be only rarely used: they often lead to inflated rumours, even when there is no truth in an allegation. It is better to be prepared for enquiries – and a good idea to rehearse strategies in the face of a range of unpleasant scenarios.

Often the first intimation of trouble will be a phone call, sometimes on a topic known to the school but sometimes a totally new story. The school must have a procedure to cope with press and broadcasting enquiries, and the telephonists must be clear to whom phone enquiries should be put through. Preferably this should always be to a senior person, for the word of the Head or a Deputy is needed to give what will be taken as an authoritative reaction. No one must give, however inadvertently, the impression that the school is stalling or that the Head is deliberately keeping away from the phone.

■ 'No comment' never works

The person who responds must never say 'No comment'. It almost always both arouses suspicion in the mind of the journalist and looks sinister if printed:

> 'When asked how it was that a boy fell from the roof of the school, Mr Charles the Headmaster was unable to comment.'

If quoted in the paper, the phrase sounds at best incompetent and more likely downright devious. If the school's spokesperson does not know about the allegation, claim as calmly as possible the need for time to investigate and call the enquirer back. Ask for as much detail as the enquirer knows about the alleged event or situation, and, of course, her or his name, publication, and number. To be helpful, and to ensure that your timing does not get translated into a 'no comment was available', check the enquirer's deadline: 'When do you need these details for press?'

■ Take care

A problem can come from the spokesperson's lack of knowledge: although such ignorance may be perfectly reasonable, ignorance of certain events can be presented in a newspaper story as an implied incompetence.

When the LEA was introducing a new contract-cleaning scheme and the outline had been published in a committee paper and agreed by the relevant LEA committee, a local paper phoned to ask my views as a Headteacher. I had not read the committee papers and had not studied the relevant legislation. Because I do not like giving views on matter I have not properly considered, I spoke truthfully, saying that I had not checked the facts and had no views. Wrongly, I thought that would be the end of the enquiry. The newspaper account, although one could not complain about inaccurate reporting, made me look foolish:

'Local Headteacher declared he knew nothing about the scheme.'

If the cause of the enquiry is, say, an accident, ignorance can sound even worse:

'Thirty minutes after last week's explosion at Downsview School, the Headteacher still did not know what had happened, although ambulances were on their way to the injured.'

However, it is possible to hold back without giving misleading impressions: 'May I ask what you have been told?' 'Yes, sadly there has been an accident; you have not been entirely accurately informed; we are investigating and taking action already. Will it be in time for your deadline if I phone back in fifteen minutes?'

Do not let the reporter tell you his or her version of what you have said: 'So, Headmistress, you are saying that...' Your reply has to be firmly but warmly: 'No, not at all: what I have said is...'

Where there has been error, admit it without unnecessary excuses, but with a brief but firm statement of intent:

```
    'The school regrets that the necessary checks
had not been made on the electrical conduits and
safety trip-switch, but new routines have at once
been initiated so that an accident like this
cannot happen again.'
```

■ Conclusion

The facts need urgent investigation and clear admission. Those who need to know include pupils, staff, parents, governors, and LEA officers. On the one hand all these people deserve the facts, and on the other their support, based on the truth, is a great force for modifying exaggerated rumour. For instance, an immediate circular letter to parents setting the record straight is usually wise after any crisis.

For the well-presented school, the occasional mishap which is well investigated, responded to, and reported will be subordinated to the range of positive events reported.

9 Using the school environment

A striking example of the underlying thesis of this book (that marketing efforts are integral to and can actually improve the central educational offer) is the environment of the school. There is virtually nothing that marketing might suggest that would not in anyway be desirable. Those aspects of a school's environment that militate against effective marketing are in almost every case a weak or positively bad contribution to the pupils' education and the school's service to its families.

This will not always or readily be agreed by staff. Indeed, generations of teachers have been forced by their conditions to become so inured to the characterless, the half-clean, and the downright shabby that they hardly look at the school environment. The pressure of a school week and the severely limited support staff establishment lead to taking nothingness and a bland emptiness for granted. This attitude is exacerbated by the underlying assumption that the pupils have to be there, and the teachers' teaching is all.

Many notices on doors in schools are poorly drafted, oddly printed, and strangely displayed. The Headteacher's door in one major school had stripes of damaged paint where a notice had been sellotaped (that great enemy of school woodwork and walls!) and removed – taking the paint with it. I have never won the battle against the remnants of the decorations of previous Christmases, just lingering with a tatty bit of red crêpe paper here and mysterious bit of silver there. It is as if there is no one in charge of the details of the fabric of some buildings. They are 'cleaned' but the cleaning is not part of a total approach to the aesthetics of a building.

No teacher should have to teach or pupil study in a dull and shabby environment. Such an environment in its turn may repulse visitors.

Few of us in schools have had the experience of working in organisations and services which have to *attract* clients to carry out their prime task. Hotels, restaurants, galleries, and theatres, for instance, do not merely require a pleasing environment to 'sell' their goods: the environment is actually part of what they are selling. That is in fact true of schools. Any decent set of school aims and any curriculum description of integrity will have aims and objectives which need supporting and even delivering by a vivid, pleasing, and comfortable environment.

Similarly, the procedures, events, and ceremonies of a school do their job better by the school's clients – both pupils and parents – if they are planned to attract outsiders.

■ The building and its displays

Architecture and interior design speak. They speak to the school community itself, reflecting back to students and staff its purpose, style, and ambition. And they speak to parents, professional visitors, and members of the communities the school serves. What messages do most schools give?

Although at the time we were very proud of the new schools of the fifties, very few post-war school buildings appear impressive now. Indeed, those of the sixties are often depressingly shabby in their main fabric. The educators of the period had little notion of pastoral care and limited expectations of home/school liaison, relationships with the community, or the need to receive visitors. The task of parents was to provide the children, not to visit the school, and there was literally and metaphorically no *place* for parents.

A further lack of most 'reception' and public areas in schools is display opportunities. A meagre but would-be impressive glass-fronted cabinet for silver-plated trophies is the usual concession to presentation, with little sign of the school's visual, design, and literary arts.

Finally, there are still schools in which it is far from clear where visitors are to go, and in which signs are either lacking or confusing. Sometimes they are positively offensive 'Visitors must report to...' There is often a muddle of styles and a scatter of poorly home-made notices.

Architects of school buildings have had adequate briefs for specialist teaching accommodation, so that our new laboratories, technology, and drama spaces are largely good, but they have had inadequate briefing for pastoral care, home/school liaison, and the public presence of the school, its need to present itself to itself and to the public, and its relationship to the communities it serves. To market itself for the future, a school has to re-consider the function of its public spaces and how they can be used to project the atmosphere and work of the school.

■ Announcing the school to the area

The functions of the main entrance and its associated public spaces include:

- announcing the school to the area;
- signalling the way in;
- welcoming visitors, and providing car parking;
- providing a receptionist in an appropriate area;
- providing a waiting area and interview rooms;
- displaying both pupil work and adult art.

■ Signing

LEA-issued school notice boards are frequently inappropriate in style and inadequate in size, number, and location. Whilst the standard LEA board will probably have to be retained in most areas, the school should consider what kind of sign is appropriate for its architecture and its area. Clearly, rural schools will have different kinds of signs from urban schools. In streetscapes the conventions of sign styles for urban areas can be followed, and large signs on a facade, appropriately illuminated, often work extremely well. The style of all signs should, if possible, incorporate the house-style of the typography established by the school and logo. This announcement of itself to the area is practical, in that the visitor can be caught when approaching the school and led by additional signs to the main entrance; it can also speak to passers-by of the pride of the school and its character.

■ Welcoming visitors

From the outer entrance of the school, parents and visitors need to be led in by adequate but not over-fussy sign systems to the reception desk. Once the visitor is within the school, there needs to be a coherent sign system, using the school house-style, which points the routes to the key places. The routes should be as convenient and as pleasant as possible. Walls, floor surfaces, planting, and decorations should all be judged from the point of view of their impact on the visitor and their statement about the standards and the aesthetic levels of the school. In multi-lingual areas there should be recognition of the linguistic diversity in translations of the signs.

Car parking is often difficult, as most schools were built to schedules on a low ratio of cars to staff. Often car parking is infuriatingly confused in school grounds, and even successful parking is followed by perplexity about the pedestrian route out of the car parks. Access to and out of the car park should be well signposted.

■ A receptionist in an appropriate area

As Headteacher I have had to commission reception offices in four school buildings. On one occasion the then ILEA responded to a request by asking: 'What is meant by a reception office?'

It is probable that in all but the largest schools the member of the office staff responsible for reception will have other duties as well, probably including the telephone switchboard and a diversity of clerical duties. Too often, this means that member of the office staff is in an inner sanctum, and the only communication with the entrance hall is through an unmarked and an unwelcoming window. Indeed, there are even some entrance halls where only a blank wooden door, perhaps with a sign, provides communication.

The first requirement is that the reception window, suitably signed and suitably illuminated, should be in a style which both suits the basic architecture of the building and also stands out as a separate reception window. This should be in a place which is neither too busy nor too isolated, and should allow a work station for the office worker inside, so that he or she can be always at reception and yet able to continue with other work. There needs to be a shelf large enough for papers on the outside and easy communication with the receptionist inside.

In my experience it is well worth employing an architect with an interest in this kind of work to survey the present entrances and offer possible solutions to the school's architectural brief. It is, of course, possible to design the work and carry it through oneself, but an architect brings professional skills and usually adds a dimension unperceived by lay people. Figures 11A and 11B show one such conversion by Culum and Nightingale.

Figure 11A   North Westminster School reception area conversion

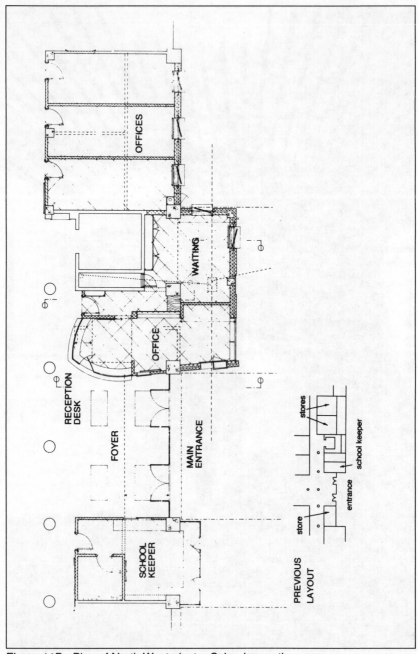

Figure 11B   Plan of North Westminster School reception area

■ Providing a waiting area

Although foyers themselves can be appropriate for waiting, they are frequently too public and too busy. The paradox of designing a waiting area is that on the one hand it is good for visitors to be within the atmosphere of the school, but on the other hand they often require privacy. For instance, a father and mother coming to talk to a member of the pastoral staff about hopes for the future, or worries about the present, want to have a certain degree of privacy.

In my view, there should ideally be both some informal waiting spaces with seating in the main foyer, where the atmosphere of the school and its artwork can be savoured, but also some more semi-private waiting in a specially designed waiting room. Such a waiting area needs to be adjacent to reception, so that the receptionists can keep reasonable communication and the visitors are not left to feel abandoned. It should also have sufficient privacy for visitors to talk and relax. Of course, the waiting room should have examples of pupils' work, and appropriate publications, such as literary anthologies by pupils.

■ Providing interview rooms

There are frequently inadequate offices for pastoral team leaders, but ideally not only Heads and Deputy Heads but also pastoral team leaders should have pleasant offices which are large enough for a working area and also a talking area, where meetings with families can be held round a table rather than across a desk. Ideally these should be close to the main concourse, so that reception, waiting room, and pastoral offices are pleasantly linked.

Even less commonly provided is an interview room. In an effective and busy school there will be a number of occasions when members of staff, who do not themselves have the privilege of their own office, will need to speak to a visitor, and if it is at all possible it is worth providing a suitably furnished and decorated interview room for these teachers and their visitors.

■ The Head's and Deputy Head's offices

It seems almost impertinent to make recommendations about other people's offices, but the contents and decorations of Head's and Deputy Head's offices do speak of the school to visitors. Many are rather vacant, and I have seen a number which are depressingly shabby, crammed with cardboard boxes, and symbolic of confusion. I like to make a point of having my offices speak of my interests and of those of the school, with a large collection of my own books, a mixture of pupils' and professional artwork, and an attempt to create a decor which speaks of the style of personal approach and aesthetic sensitivity that should be the hallmark of the school.

■ Displaying pupil work and adult art

The fabric, design, and displays in schools can help deliver the curriculum to the pupil. For instance, a school that includes in its curriculum ambitions to bring a range of visual arts of different genre and cultural traditions to the pupils would clearly wish to have displays not only of the pupils' own work, but also of professional artists. In my own school we have a separate budget heading for arts displays, and exhibitions range from modern art of Nigeria through to Islamic book binding and the work of local artists. From a curriculum point of view such displays can be both a specific part of the taught curriculum, in that classes are brought with teachers to look at and discuss the work, but, equally importantly, are also seen as part of the planned but undirected curriculum, at which pupils look in their own time, of their own volition, with different degrees of interest.

Displays in a school are obviously important in projecting the values of the school to visitors. A school's aesthetic interest can be conveyed through the displays in its public places. There are many schools where good work is done in visual arts, design, technology, and English literature, but these activities are locked up in their own classrooms. How much better that the public spaces should be used to display them. Such displays should not merely be on pinboards: pictures should be properly framed or glazed, adult work should mix with student work, and there should be appropriately illuminated display cabinets for three-dimensional objects.

■ Teaching spaces

Similarly, in our art-starved schools, many classrooms are barren visually. Indeed, some are positively shabby. As visitors and parents look round a school, the impressions of the details of the classroom environment mean a great deal – as they do to the self-esteem and interest of the pupils working in them.

Many corridors, and schools often have to have many corridors, are very empty, but could have regularly changed art displays. A good architect can often see ways of improving the effect of the circulation spaces. For instance, it is sometimes possible to build in glass-fronted book display cabinets and find other ways of bringing artifacts and interesting historical displays to the pupils' and visitors' attention.

■ Conclusion

It is possible, not only to keep schools clean and pleasant, but also to make the major areas interesting to members of the school's own community and to visitors. To do so requires a personal touch, to make use of the school's artistic, cultural, and social life, and to invest in the fabric of the building and its displays. Such activities are not merely superficial 'decoration', but grow out of the teaching activity and feed back into it, at the same time vigorously marketing the work of the school to visitors.

10 Meeting parents and visitors

In any organisation the manner in which every member of the staff relates to the clients is a major part of the impression that is given of the concern, skill, and effectiveness of the organisation. This is doubly so if the prime purpose of the organisation is concerned with the welfare of people in any way. Being careless about this is bad enough if an organisation is, say, an electrical wholesaler, but if it is a counselling service, a hospital, or a school, the mismatch between aims and style of relationship lead to a poor regard by the clients of the professional service being provided.

Regrettably, the work of a school is often so rushed that there is little or no planned time for relating to parents, the community, or the local media. More than that, though, many teachers, shaped by years of heavy classroom work, have had little experience of communicating professionally with adults outside teaching. I have seen time and again unsmiling encounters, lacking the courtesy of an introduction, and abruptly handled. 'What's the problem?' was the terse opening remark I heard from one senior teacher to a nervous-looking parent.

Fairly often parents find even in 'Parents' Evenings' that teachers treat them off-handedly. As teacher after teacher criticises their child, parents can become deeply depressed. As teacher after teacher is touchily defensive, parents become confused and irritated.

Office staff too are often very busy and badly located in crowded offices. However, the problems are wider than that: they are rarely if ever adequately briefed, still less trained. Their counterparts in IBM, Rank Hotels, or any major commercial organisation will have had proper training in that part of their job which is public relations. There are many good people working well, but I fear also many occasions of surprised-looking staff, apparently not expecting, still less welcoming, the visitor. Far too often, there is even rudeness and misunderstanding.

◾ Introductions

The importance of introductions cannot be over-emphasised but is often overlooked in schools. Even if a boy does explain to his father: 'Dad, this is my Maths teacher', that teacher should stand, shake hands, and introduce himself: 'Hallo, Mr Brown. It's good to meet you. I'm Charles Jones, and I teach John's maths course'.

◾ Badges

For specially convened general meetings, when there are many staff around, badges are a help. Specially designed (with the school logo) self-adhesive badges can be worn on lapels.

◾ Cards

Strangely, 'business cards' are rarely used in schools, unlike every other walk of professional life and unlike schools in, say, the USA. I recommend that a school should provide cards for its pastoral and senior management at least. Personally, I always carry my cards, and give one to every parent or visitor whom I meet for the first time – and the cards carry my home phone number.

◾ Training

The school's relationship with parents and other visitors is *part of its task*, not only a means towards it. There should be conscious policy and even training to help all concerned to relate to parents. A seminar with a small group of parents describing how they felt when at parents' meetings can prompt a greater sensitivity.

Simulations, videos, and feed-back from parents and visitors can be used for professional development. None of us like our 'personal style' commented on, but we need a mirror held up to ourselves. Facial expressions (such as a worried frown), body language (such as an over-relaxed or an aggressive stance), or an oral style can confuse, distress, and put off parents. These aspects of professional behaviour are part of the work of the school, and are amenable to professional monitoring, training, and substantial change.

■ Conclusion

Warm, personal, and professionally competent relationships are not only an obligation as part of the education of pupils and our working with the communities of the area, but also a vital and powerful aspect of marketing. There will be strong impressions circulating among parents simply on how they are spoken to. Every word spoken speaks for the school. In addition to the immediate purpose of the conversation, the spoken style will have contributed to the image of the school and thus to its marketing.

11 Making the most of school events

All schools meet their broader curriculum aims by devising a variety of events outside the timetabled courses (or 'subjects') which complement those courses. In many schools there is a very rich programme of events which grows out of the curriculum and feeds back to the cultural life of the school. These events cannot only be made part of the marketing strategy at no loss to themselves, but, and this is most important to stress, can benefit from that strategy. The conversion of a school event into a public event in itself adds an interest for the students and gives the project a boost.

For instance, as part of the professional development and the In-service work at North Westminster School, we have endeavoured to have a number of visiting educational specialists leading seminars and workshops and giving presentations. Once a year, funding has been found from an outside body, for the first eight years IBM, for the 'IBM/North Westminster Annual Education Lecture'. Making this public, raised funds to pay for an outstanding speaker, and *added a prestige* to the event which made it easier to attract speakers. From a 'marketing' point of view, this made it possible to present the event to the world and to attract others into the audience.

Similarly, when we have an arts exhibition, we have a public opening, with a notable speaker. This allows students to mix with visitors and take part in the presentation. It gives a sense of occasion to those who have prepared the exhibition, and *it presents one of the artistic faces of the school to the world.*

There is a wide range of possibilities for events which combine curriculum delivery, communal life, and external presentation: sporting events, visiting performers, school performances, exhibitions, and ceremonies noting and commemorating local historical and cultural events. For instance, the centenary of the local church can be marked by an event with historical readings, literature, music, and art of the period. When the statue of Sarah Siddons on the green of Paddington church near our Upper School was restored, we had an evening celebration, with a lecture on Sarah Siddons' life by an academic, and slides about her work with students performing the key speeches.

■ 'Awards Evenings' and 'Open Days'

Many schools have adapted the traditional 'Prize Day' event to make it more of a celebration. I have also seen a number of those in recent years which were 'performances' in themselves. Figure 12 shows a programme from one of my own school's 'Awards Evenings', in which not only are prizes and certificates given away, but most significantly awards are given for a range of activities, and carefully worded citations read out to describe the achievement of each. This both better rewards the individual and her or his family by a closer description of the achievement, and makes a fuller public statement.

The choosing of visitors to speak and give away such rewards is important for the contribution to the curriculum of the school, symbolising achievement in one world or another, and makes a public statement of the importance of the school's work. Of course the finest statement of all is to have a former student of the school who has 'made it' – or is on the way to doing so – in the world.

If there is a good art display on, and there are literary, musical, and dance performances as part of the evening, not only does it make it a better event for those there, and a fuller celebration for the work of the school, but it makes a fuller and more vivid statement to community members invited. Tape-slide presentations of, for instance, crafts and design work can fit in excellently to such a programme.

A number of schools have annual 'Open Days', and these are obviously a good opportunity to show the work of the school. They demand a lot of work from many staff, and the artificiality of trying to show ordinary classwork creates problems – inevitably the visitors see more of other visitors than they do of the ordinary work. They can, however, be devised most successfully.

It is also possible to have more small-scale visits, in which pupils take two or three visitors around the school at a time. A school in southern England found this approach substantially increased pupil numbers. In a well-run school with a pleasant atmosphere, this is one of the most powerful statements about its work that can be made, and the most effective way of 'marketing'. It also provides excellent experience for the pupil guides.

1 · 9 · 9 · 0
AWARDS

Upper School   7.00 pm   Wednesday 7th November 1990

Guest of Honour
Heather Couper
Astronomer and Television Broadcaster

1 The Next Decade
The Headteacher's Report: Professor Michael Marland CBE MA

2 Mazurka (opus 67, No. 44)
Frederic Chopin (1810 - 1849) arranged by A W Benoy
Glow-Anne Crawford (flute), Andrei Morgan (flute), Alice Turner (clarinet),
Sachiel Dunn (clarinet)

3 Presentation of Examiation Certificates
Examinations Administrator: Jerry Hicken   Director of Curriculum: Mick Hornsby

4 Polka
Charles d'Albert (1864 - 1932)

5 Presentation of Awards
Heads of Houses: Anna Dolezal and Audrey Sansom
Director of Upper School: Lynn Gadd

6 Mars from The Planets
Gustav Holst (1874 - 1934)
Choreography : Royston Muldoon, by arrangement with the Royal Ballet
Dancers: Nozil Ahmed, Carleta Barrett, Sweea Blesky, Susan Bryan, Alison Burke,
Caroline Charter, Jocelyn Dyett, Millicent Frimpong, Kalina Georgieva, Robin Hanson, Anhar Miah, Belen
Moar, Carmen Moar, Serena McKenzie, Sana Mouziane

7 Guest of Honour: Helen Couper

8 Chaos
Music: Vim   Choreography: David Steel
North West Dance: Mounira Almenoar, Melissa Beal, Nicole Butcher,
Caroline Charter, Sean Gaffney, Asma Ibnahaten, Samira Saleem
Dance Performances directed by Michele Inniss
North West Dance partially funded by Greater London Arts

* * * * * *

Production Managers : Armando da Silva, Peter West
The performance directed by the Director of the Studio Theatre: Mark Pattenden
and Head of Performing Arts: Debbie Goldman
Stage Crew: Gloria Akinyemi, Aicha Attouka, Paul Burton, Nicky Carter,
Giovanna Capaluongo, Jay Cochrane, Glow-Anne Crawford, Kevin Crawford,
Mathew Hanson, Amy Mortimer, Simon Mudge, Dayo Zabat

Figure 12   A programme from a North Westminster School Awards
Evening

AWARD WINNERS

Paddington Rotary Club Award for Community Service
Afshin Kanji

Marylebone Rotary Club Award for Community Service
Amin Belal

Tutor Group Awards
Marylebone 6th
Binh Ly 6Ml; Fatimot Bello 6M2; Amelia Critchlow, Che Porteus 6M3; Colleen Douglas, Ahamadour Choudhury6M4; Joanne Burwood, Charles Amirmansour U6Ml; Leyla Mroueh U6M2
Paddington 6th
Mustapha Hasnaoui 6Pl; Lila McMahon 6P2; Rohinee Someseggaram 6P4; Priti Patel, Vafa Jamnezhad U6P
Marylebone 5th
Khola Tufail 5M1; Nasima Begum 5M2; Lisa Melville 5M3; Po Yee Ho 5M4;
Jenny Brandrith 5M5; Laura McManus 5M6
Paddington 5th
Reem Samara 5P2; Fatima Begum, Fiona Haar 5P3; Raquib Miah 5P4;
Revathy Sommasagaram, Roshan Hannan 5P5

Siggismund Goetze Awards for Artistic Achievement
Overall Artistic Achievement: Michelle Tute; Home Studies: Nikeeta Vagh;
Performing Arts
Dance: Lorna McCann, Mahani Dean; Drama: Katey Edwards; Music: Wayne Tute
Visual Arts
Alison Barry, Raymond Andaya; Media: Nida Fernandcz; Fabric: Nasima Begum,Hasna Bibi

Achievement in Physical Education
AmyLamont 5M5; Shahed Mohammed Yunus 6Pl

Academic Achievement
Chemistry: Joshua Hierro 5Pl; Physics: Sadie Arora 5P4; Biology: Vimlesh Maru U6M2;
English: Sin Wen Tse 5M6, Catey Edwards U6M2;
Child Development: Lisa Mellille 5M3; I.T: Vijaya Rohinee Somasegaram 6P4;
Maths: Hasna Bibi 5P6, Fiona Haar 5P3; CDT: Sam Hurt 5M3, Kourosh Ahmadi 5P3
French & Spanish: Rita Coyne U6P; Spanish: Caroline WoodU6M2; Italian: Carla Ballard 5P2;
German: Emma Doran 5M5; Bengali: Nozmul Mahmud 6M; Arabic: Hasna Bibi 5P6 History:
Shamsun Nehar-Khanom 5M5, Patrick Bitakanamire U6P;
Geography: Rowshan Hannan 6P5; Sociology: Ghulam Rabbani 5M6; Farhana Bari 5P4;
Learning Support: Shelley Nessa 5M3, Jason Byrnes 5P6; Business Studies: Elizabeth Bowyer U6M2;
E.S.L.: Dilara Begum 5M4, STaS: Nasima Begum 5M2, Bonnie Bloch 5P2;

Certificate of Pre-Vocational Education
Business & Administration: Colleen Douglas 6M4;
General Course: Jamaldin Bakkali 6M3; Fashion: Salaha Khatun 6P2;
Production & Technical: Rafiz Ali 6P3

Best Advanced-Level Result
Caroline Wood, Simon Chen

* * * * * * * *

Director of Upper School: Lynn Gadd; Director of Administration: Gill Thompson;
Director of Finance : Val Racher; Schoolkeeper: Peter Hayes;
Bookshop Manager: Sereta Boyle

North Westminster Community School

▮ Outside events

Although difficult to organise, visits by students to take part in external events and demonstrations of their work can be extremely effective. These may be performing groups but can also include static exhibitions of pupils' artwork or photographs of them at work.

With imagination, effort, and good organisation, it is possible to enrich and extend the full range of learning activities of a school so that pupils themselves benefit, and so that strong statements are made to the outside world. A review of the marketing value of the full range of events is part of a coherent programme.

12 Sponsorship and working with businesses

In a Sussex school, a building society paid for the refurbishment of a room used by parents and pupils in return for displaying leaflets and advertisements in the room.

Schools in Kent agreed a deal with the county council and an advertising agency to allow poster advertising on school sites in exchange for a regular cash sum.

In an Essex school, a financial services company gives advice to staff and provides experts to talk to business studies classes. A banner advertising the company is erected at major school events, and the school gets a share of the profits made by the company selling mortgages and insurance policies to the teachers.

A Milton Keynes school receives £1 for every pupil who opens an account at a local bank.

This is sponsorship – and organised carefully and, as far as possible, on equal terms with the sponsoring company, it can bring useful benefits to a school.

Sponsorship, according to *The Economist's Pocket Guide to Marketing*, is the subsidising of an event by a company for advertising purposes. The company's aims are to achieve wide coverage, to associate it or its product with a pleasurable experience, and to promote its corporate image.

▪ The two sides of sponsorship

But what's in it for a school? Sponsorship can:

- provide new sources of funds for the school;

- deliver other resources such as advice and expertise, work experience opportunities, and new equipment;

- supply targeted backing for specific activities, such as the production of a school brochure, a signing system for the school, and reclaiming or renovating a derelict or under-utilised area of the school;

- build a two-way relationship between school and local business and industry;

- attract media and public attention to school activities and developments.

Yet there is often considerable suspicion about sponsorship. For some it has dubious ethical and moral implications. It smacks too much of being used for propaganda purposes. What you 'give away' is never matched by the return. Advertising pervades everywhere; why should it come into schools too?

All these objections have some truth in them. Examples can be cited of schools being 'ripped off' or taken for a ride. In its advice to members on sponsorship, the National Union of Teachers cites examples of 'unfair' practices – a school governor setting up a sponsorship deal with a company of which she was chief executive; banks negotiating monopolies on a school site so that pupils do not have a choice of where to open an account; school-site posters that advertise products banned in a school; commercially-sponsored educational material that is biased and inaccurate.

But the lesson to be learnt is not that sponsorship should be avoided, but rather that the school should:

- develop a proper policy on sponsorship agreed between all groups in the school community (staff, governors, parents, and pupils) with criteria that deal with the concerns about sponsorship in a positive way;

- provide a suitable formula for negotiating a sponsorship deal within the aims and values of the school.

Many of the horror stories recounted about schools and sponsorship are echoes of what was happening in the arts world when it took the sponsorship route several years ago. Practical experience, exchange of ideas, training courses, and the development of codes of practice and guidelines by national arts and marketing organisations have brought a well-honed professionalism to the dealings between arts companies and commercial sponsors. The same is beginning to happen with the education world.

Sponsorship is not charity or patronage. It is, or should be, a proper business arrangement from which both sides benefit on the terms and to the extent that they want and which is reasonable in relation to what is on offer by each side.

Today, arts companies are better at, and happier with, sponsorship precisely because they have worked out their own policy on what they want, what they will accept and what they will not. It puts them on more equal terms with a potential sponsor.

The Association for Business Sponsorship of the Arts (ABSA) has produced a set of principles for good practice in arts sponsorship *Setting Standards for the 1990s*. It provides some valuable advice for schools:

▶ **'The common interest between sponsor and sponsored demands that their relationship be based on mutual respect, candour and understanding, with each investing the necessary time and attention to define clearly the aims of the sponsorship, the expectations of the deal, and the provisions for evaluating and publicising projects. They must also attempt to understand the other's motivation.'**

■ Agreeing a policy

All groups in a school should discuss their attitudes to sponsorship – its advantages and disadvantages, its risks and opportunities, what is acceptable and what is not – and agree a policy for the school through the governing body.

Issues to consider include:

1 Why do you want sponsorship and what can you gain from it?

2 What can you offer potential sponsors?

3 What are the ethical and practical issues? (the two can overlap)

   They can be:

   • type of product made by a company;

   • its public reputation;

   • its interests in other countries;

   • its commercial or political activities;

   • type and location of advertising;

   • age range of pupils targeted by any advertising;

   • events or activities to be linked to sponsorship or created specifically for sponsorship;

- a sponsor's involvement with the school curriculum;

- use of company name and logo: (when, where, and what size?);

- number of sponsors and length of agreements.

In some cases, a general rule might be made, such as no tobacco or brewing companies, or no company operating in countries under a United Nations trade embargo or creating unacceptable environmental damage. In others, issues may arise when specific sponsorship is being considered.

Some issues may not be very clear cut, for example, concerns at the health consequences of various food products, or conflicting evidence of a company's industrial processes or of the effects of its products. It might be useful to appoint someone or a small group of people drawn from parents, teachers, governors and pupils to act as a sponsorship research team to identify potential sponsors that meet the school's agreed criteria, and to check out their 'suitability' and that of companies which make a direct approach to the school.

With the plethora of special interest and pressure groups, schools will have to tread a careful path between extremes which see all economic processes and commercial activities as suspect, and those who uncritically consider all such activity as legitimate. There will obviously be grey areas. Since a school does not have the resources for detailed investigations or the expertise to assess often highly technical evidence, it may have to live with inconsistencies.

A well-debated, agreed and clearly set-out policy will give a school the confidence not to be panicked into precipitating action either way, and to act decisively when required. One useful yardstick is to ask what message will be conveyed to pupils by the acceptance or rejection of a particular sponsor.

■ A positive policy

Make any sponsorship policy as positive as possible. You want to attract the right sponsors not frighten them off – it is easy to spot a reluctant partner.

Seek to fit sponsorship opportunities and benefits within the way the school works – or wishes to work – and how you market the school as a whole. Do not change the school's aims and beliefs to meet what you perceive to be sponsors' requirements. This is not to suggest that nothing must change. There will be organisational changes, new or redeveloped activities and opportunities. (Why else do you want the sponsorship?)

In any policy document, set out the school's aims and beliefs and relate the sponsorship to them. This makes clear that the school is interested in sponsorship for the opportunities it can create to fulfil those aims. List the advantages perceived for both sides followed by the limits that are to be set.

The mere existence of a written and detailed sponsorship policy will tell any company that you mean business. On the one hand, this will discourage those that feel a school is a soft touch; on the other, it will encourage those that are after a professional, mutually beneficial sponsorship deal.

Once agreed, consider launching the sponsorship policy by releasing it to the press (see **Writing press releases** on pages 58-61).

■ Negotiating a sponsorship deal

Experience has shown that these guidelines will help you to make a beneficial deal:

- **Be open with your sponsor**: show your enthusiasm for a good relationship, state your aims and what areas are *not* open to negotiation. Indicate that you expect a similar level of openness and good intent from the sponsor. It is best to know early on where sponsor and school do not see eye-to-eye.

- **Appoint a main negotiator** to represent the school and make clear where the final decisions are made.

- **Agree a timetable** for negotiation and for implementing agreed proposals.

- **Decide how long you want an agreement to run**. This is likely to be a negotiating point with an agreement based on an initial 'running-in' period, options to confirm and renew agreements, and stating the period of notice required for ending an agreement.

- **All agreements with a sponsor should be in writing**. You may need to seal the final agreement with a formal exchange of contract.

- **Make sure that agreements do not conflict** where the school has more than one sponsor.

- **Make clear** what sort of products and services the school will promote (e.g. those which match educational ideals).

- **Do not make assumptions about what companies will sponsor.**
  The majority of sponsors want to support conventional areas of
  activity. But a large, and growing, number also like to be seen to
  be backing innovative or controversial aspects of an
  organisation, as the arts world has found out. It may be harder
  to find sponsors for such work but they do exist.

- **Make sure there are no conflicts of interest** within the school,
  such as teachers or governors, or between the school and other
  schools in the area. (The Education (School Government)
  Regulations 1989 states that *any* person at a governing body
  meeting (not just governors) must declare a direct or indirect
  pecuniary interest where a contract or other matter is to be
  discussed. She or he must not take part in the discussions, must
  withdraw from the meeting unless the governing body allow
  otherwise, and must not write on the issue concerned.)

■ Curriculum involvement

A growing number of sponsorships offer schools the opportunity to
give their pupils work experience with the sponsoring companies and
access to new equipment in the classroom. Any such sponsor would
naturally take a keen interest in the school's curriculum. A school
needs to decide when interest becomes interference.

Business and industry have an increasingly legitimate interest in
what schools teach and pupils learn. (See **Working with businesses**
on pages 101-102). Discussing the curriculum and suggesting how
improvements can be made or helping schools better meet national
curriculum demands by providing additional resources, funding or
materials should not, in itself, be seen as interference.

The National Consumer Council has produced a set of guidelines for
business sponsors of educational material, and no serious sponsor
would object to agree to such arrangements:

- Any educational material that is sponsored should be clearly
  listed as such.

- Promotional material should not be designated as educational.

- Sponsors should not distribute or direct-mail unsolicited material
  to pupils or parents.

- Headteachers and governors should have the right to control
  what material is given to pupils on behalf of sponsors.

Such material should:

- be assessed by the relevant teachers and able to meet pupils' curriculum needs as agreed by the school;

- be sensitive to the needs and expectations of all groups likely to receive it;

- reflect as far as possible the races, cultures, and lifestyles within the community;

- avoid sexual and racial stereotyping;

- promote self-esteem in each pupil.

■ Evaluating a sponsorship

Assessing how a sponsorship is going – and has gone – will help you to plan future sponsorship deals with more confidence and to the school's greater benefit.

It is worth considering whether to evaluate a sponsorship arrangement as it is proceeding, as well as at the end of its run.

Appoint a member of the school (teacher, governor, parent) to:

- monitor progress;

- liaise with the sponsor;

- boost awareness and interest within the school community;

- identify difficulties in carrying out the agreement with the sponsor;

- encourage feedback from the school and outside about the sponsorship and its effects.

As a sponsorship is coming to an end or coming up for renewal, you need to decide if the arrangement has delivered what you want in the way you want it.

- What have been the benefits to the school?

- Is the sponsor happy with the outcome?

- What problems arose for school and sponsor?

- How can future sponsorships be improved?

■ Working with businesses

Schools and businesses get together because they see that each has benefits for the other. Apart from helping through sponsorship businesses can offer:

- work experience and work-shadowing opportunities;
- involvement in governing bodies;
- opportunities for teachers to work in business;
- personnel to work with schools;
- specialist equipment;
- projects for pupils to become familiar with business techniques and activities;
- job opportunities in return for agreed levels of attainment in key attributes such as literacy, numeracy, and social skills, including good attendance and punctuality.

But businesses will be looking for certain key elements in the life of a school when considering any kind of partnership such as a sponsorship arrangement. Research by the Confederation of British Industry (CBI) shows that businesses are concerned that:

- pupils develop basic skills such as communication, literacy and numeracy, screen and keyboard, inter-personal and life, and problem-solving skills;
- pupils display a broad knowledge of subjects ranging across maths, science, languages, humanities, and economic awareness;
- pupils are motivated and have positive attitudes in life and work;
- staff show sound management in the way they run the school.

In turn, schools expect that business should:

- understand what a school is seeking to achieve and support it;
- involve itself with the school and show commitment to its aims and values;
- provide experience of the world of work;
- develop a partnership which involves school/industry liaison committees, curriculum-working parties, industrial tutors, setting up 'real-world' projects for pupils, and putting forward managers and directors for the school governing body.

Any form of partnership will cost time, but will also take a place in the overall plan. There is an understandable tendency for those in schools to look too guardedly and too narrowly at the gains a commercial organisation would hope to obtain from such links. In my experience much of the motive is essentially altruistic – especially sheer interest in the welfare of the young.

Pupils often gain a sense of additional approbation from the sponsorship of an established firm. Similarly, the 'goodwill' bought by a firm via its investment in a school activity is balanced, if not far exceeded, by the public relations projection for the school into the community.

13 The projecting school

The node of power for school planning since the 1986 and 1988 Acts has been the governing body. The United Kingdom school system has moved from 'a national system locally administered', as the conventional wisdom called the post-1944 dispensation of power, to a school-based system monitored locally against national criteria, as I should describe the post-1988 dispensation. It is the governors and the Head who agree the aims for the school, modify or accept the LEA curriculum policy, establish its curriculum (against the requirements of Section 1 of the 1988 Act and incorporating the elements known as the National Curriculum), and are responsible for a staffing structure and policies to deliver that.

In doing this, the governors and the Head are bound by statute as well as by the climate of society to be responsive to the aspirations of the communities they serve and the parents (the school's legal clients) and their children (the school's students).

Highly idealistic as the criteria of Section 1 of the *Education Act 1988* are, and as apparently demanding and precise as the National Curriculum elements are, the scope for each school to establish its own persona, style, and organisational approach is immense. If a school can demonstrate it meets national criteria and the LEA curriculum policy, there are few restraints other than those of the size of the delegated budget.

In this context, a school gains strength by its creative interaction with parents and the communities it serves. It has to analyse external requirements, sensitise itself, adjust, and develop as required. Both to do this, and to communicate with its communities and clients, it has to create a portrait of itself and convey that portrait to others. This process is known as marketing, but it is not something merely done to the 'product' of the school, but is rather an integral part of school development. Not only is it impossible to market a weak product successfully, but the process of marketing also enlivens the process of school self-evaluation and thus strengthens the school.

The change in attitude in schools is analogous to the change in approach by manufacturers. Robert Heller in his *The Pocket Manager* defined marketing thus:

▶ 'This busiest of buzzwords in management is used, misused, and abused by managers all over the globe. Its proper understanding is essential to modern management – and that understanding is greatly helped by knowing how the "marketing concept" emerged. It came as a reaction to the long seller's market, during which producers simply manufactured what they wanted to make – not what the market wanted. Marketing turns that obsolete concept on its head.'

In our 'market' there is far more unanimity between parents and schools than sometimes appears. (For instance the DES survey of the late eighties found 'satisfaction' figures from parents in the high 80 per cents.) However, schools still have much to learn. The long period of the 'seller's market, during which producers simply manufactured what they wanted to make – not what the market wanted' is over in schooling also.

Few schools will be able to do all that they want and the limitations of delegated budgets will always restrict. However, a school that has a coherent, vigorous, and imaginative plan for marketing will increase both the popularity and intrinsic strength of the school.

Appendix: Statutory requirements for information

Here we reproduce key parts of the *Education (No 2) Act 1986* and the *Education (School Curriculum and Related Information) Regulations 1989* which state what information schools are legally required to provide.

Acts of Parliament set down the law in general terms only. But they give powers to government departments, such as the DES, to make more detailed regulations (known as Statutory Instruments) about what, in this case, is required of headteachers, governors and local education authorities.

The DES also issues Circulars which explain Acts and Statutory Instruments – or government policy in relation to them – in more detail. While Circulars are not themselves legally binding, they are regarded as the best interpretation of how a section of an Act or a Statutory Instrument should operate in practice. Schools and local authorities *can* ignore them – but do so at their peril.

■ Education (No 2) Act 1986, section 30

1 The articles of government for every county, voluntary and maintained special school, shall provide for it to be the duty of the governing body to prepare, once in every school year, a report (the governors' report) containing:

   a) a summary of the steps taken by the governing body in the discharge of their functions during the period since their last report; and

   b) such other information as the articles may require.

2 The articles of government for every such school shall, in particular, require the governors' report:

   a) to be as brief as is reasonably consistent with the requirements as to its contents;

b) where there is an obligation on the governing body (by virtue of section 31 of this Act) to hold an annual parents' meeting:

• to give details of the date, time and place for the next such meeting and its agenda;

• to indicate that the purpose of that meeting will be to discuss both the governors' report and the discharge by the governing body, the head teacher and the local education authority, of their functions in relation to the school; and

• to report on the consideration which has been given to any resolutions passed at the previous such meeting;

c) to give the name of each governor and indicate whether he is a parent, teacher or foundation governor or was co-opted or otherwise appointed as a governor, or is an ex-officio governor;

d) to say, in the case of an appointed governor, by whom he was appointed;

e) to give, in relation to each governor who is not an ex-officio governor, the date on which his term of office comes to an end;

f) to name, and give the address of, the chairman of the governing body and their clerk;

g) to give such information as is available to the governing body about arrangements for the next election of parent governors;

h) to contain a financial statement:

• reproducing or summarising the latest financial statement provided for the governing body by the local education authority (by the virtue of paragraph (a) of section 29 (1) of this Act);

• indicating, in general terms, how any sum made available to the governing body by the authority (by virtue of paragraph (b) of that section), in the period covered by the report, was used; and

• giving details of the application of any gifts made to the school in that period;

i) to give, in the case of a secondary school, such information in relation to the public examinations as is required to be published (by virtue of section 8 (5) of the 1980 Act);

j) to describe what steps have been taken by the governing body to develop or strengthen the school's links with the community (including links with the police); and

k) to draw attention to the information made available by the governing body in accordance with the regulations made under section 20 of this Act.

3 The articles of government for every such school shall:

a) enable the governing body to produce their report in such language or languages (in addition to English) as they consider appropriate; and

b) require them to produce it in such language or languages (in addition to English and any other language in which the governing body propose to produce it) as the local education authority may direct.

4 The articles of government for every such school shall provide for it to be the duty of the governing body of any such school to take such steps as are reasonably practicable to secure that:

a) the parents of all registered pupils at the school and all persons employed at the school are given (free of charge) a copy of the governors' report;

b) copies of the report are available for inspection (at all reasonable times and free of charge) at the school; and

c) where there is an obligation on the governing body to hold an annual parents' meeting, copies of the report to be considered at that meeting are given to parents not less than two weeks before that meeting.

◼ Education (No 2) Act 1986, section 31

1 Subject to subsections 7 and 8 below, the articles of government for every county, voluntary and maintained special school shall provide for it to be the duty of the governing body to hold a meeting once in every school year ("the annual parents' meeting") which is open to:

a) all parents of registered pupils at the school;

b) the head teacher; and

c) such other persons as the governing body may invite.

2 The purpose of the meeting shall be to provide an opportunity for discussion of:

a) the governors' report; and

b) the discharge by the governing body, the head teacher and the local education authority of their functions in relation to the school.

3 No person who is not a parent of a registered pupil at the school may vote on any question put to the meeting.

4 The articles of government for every such school shall provide:

a) for the proceedings at any annual parents' meeting to be under the control of the governing body;

b) for any annual parents' meeting, at which the required number of parents of registered pupils at the school are present, to be entitled to pass (by a simple majority) resolutions on any matters which may properly be discussed at the meeting;

c) for it to be the duty of the governing body:

- to consider any resolution which is duly passed at such a meeting and which they consider is a matter for them;

- to send to the head teacher a copy of any such resolution which they consider is a matter for him; and

- to send to the local education authority a copy of any such resolution which they consider is a matter for the authority; and

d) for it to be the duty of the head teacher, and of the local education authority, to consider any such resolution a copy of which has been sent to him, or them, by the governing body and to provide the governing body with a brief comment on it (in writing) for inclusion in their next governors' report.

5 The articles of government for every county, controlled or maintained special school shall provide for any question whether any person is to be treated as the parent of a registered pupil at the school, for the purposes of any provision of the articles relating to the annual parents' meeting, to be determined by the local education authority.

6 The articles of government for every aided or special agreement school shall provide for any such question to be determined by the governing body.

7 The articles of government for every special school established in a hospital shall provide that where the governing body are of the opinion that it would be impracticable to hold an annual parents' meeting in a particular school year they may refrain from holding such a meeting in that year.

8 The articles of government for every county, voluntary and maintained special school (other than a special school established in a hospital), the proportion of registered pupils at which who are boarders is, or is likely to be, at least fifty per cent, shall provide that where:

a) the governing body are of the opinion that it would be impracticable to hold an annual parents' meeting in a particular school year; and

b) at least fifty per cent of the registered pupils at the school are boarders at the time when the governing body form that opinion;

they may refrain from holding such a meeting in that year.

9 In subsection 4b above "the required number", in relation to any school, means any number equal to at least twenty per cent of the number of registered pupils at the school.

■ Education (School Curriculum and Related Information) Regulations 1989

Information to be published with the governing body's annual report to parents and supply of copies of that report

4 (1) The governing body of every maintained school shall publish with the annual report required to be prepared under section 30 of the 1986 Act or section 58(5)(j) of the 1988 Act (as the case may be) particulars of the dates of the beginning and end of each term and of half-term holidays for the next school year and a summary of any changes to information contained in the school prospectus since it was last published.

(2) The governing body shall furnish a copy of such a report as is referred to in paragraph (1) and of the particulars and summary referred to therein to the head teacher of the school and:

a) in the case of a grant-maintained school, to the Secretary of State; and

b) in the case of any other school, to the education authority.

Public access to documents and information

5 (1) Each education authority shall furnish the governing body and the head teacher of every county, voluntary and special school maintained by them (other than a special school established in a hospital) with an up to date copy of any written statement made by them under section 17 of the 1986 Act (statement of policy in relation to the secular curriculum).

(2) The governing body of every county, controlled and maintained special school (other than a special school established in a hospital) shall furnish the head teacher and the education authority with an up to date copy of any written statement made by them pursuant to provision made under section 18(1) of the 1986 Act (statement of conclusions as to the aims of the secular curriculum for the school and how (if at all) the education authority's policy should be modified).

(3) The governing body of every aided school shall, where they have made any written statement of their policy as to the secular curriculum for the school, furnish a copy of it to the head teacher and to the education authority.

(4) The governing body of every grant-maintained school shall, where they have made any written statement of their policy as to the secular curriculum for the school, furnish a copy of it to the head teacher and the Secretary of State.

(5) Every head teacher to whom any copy of a statement is furnished under this regulation shall make it available, at all reasonable times, to persons wishing to inspect it.

6 (1) Subject to paragraph (2), the head teacher of every maintained school shall make available on request the information referred to in paragraph (3), at all reasonable times.

(2) Paragraph (1) does not apply to such information where it relates solely to a nursery class in a primary school.

(3) The information referred to in paragraph (1) is information relating to:

a) any statutory instruments, departmental circulars and administrative memoranda sent by the Department of Education and Science to the head teacher or the governing body relating to the powers and duties imposed by or under Chapter I of Part I of the 1988 Act (The Curriculum);

b) any published reports of Her Majesty's Inspectors referring expressly to the school;

c) any schemes of work currently used in the school;

d) any syllabuses followed by pupils at the school, whether for qualifications authenticated by an outside person or otherwise;

e) in the case of any county, voluntary or maintained special school (other than a special school established in a hospital), the arrangements made by the education authority under section 23 of the 1988 Act for the consideration and disposal of complaints;

f) in the case of any grant-maintained school, the arrangements made by the governing body under the school's articles of government for the consideration and disposal of complaints relating to any matter concerning the curriculum followed within the school;

g) i) in the case of any maintained school other than a grant-maintained school, any agreed syllabus for religious education adopted by the education authority which applies in that school;

ii) in the case of any voluntary school, that part of the trust deed governing religious education and any other written statement produced by the governing body about the arrangements which have been made for religious education in that school; and

iii) in the case of any grant-maintained school, such of the documents referred to in sub-paragraph (g) (i) or (ii) as apply in relation to that school.

(4) The requirement in paragraph (1) may be fulfilled by making available for inspection copies of any documents referred to in paragraph (3), or of any documents containing the information referred to therein.

7 (1) The head teacher of any maintained school shall, on request, supply a copy of any document which he is required to make available for inspection under regulation 5, and may supply a copy of any document (except those which are copyright) made available pursuant to regulation 6(4).

(2) The head teacher may make a charge (not exceeding the cost of production) in respect of any copies supplied under paragraph (1).

Explanatory note (This note is not part of the Regulations)

These Regulations impose requirements on local education authorities ('education authorities'), governing bodies and head teachers to provide information about the curriculum in county and voluntary schools, maintained special schools not established in hospitals, and grant-maintained schools (referred to in the Regulations as 'maintained schools'.) Regulation 2(2) provides that where information is required to be provided in a form specified in the Regulations, it may be supplied in computer-readable form.

Regulation 3 amends the Education (School Information) Regulations 1981 by substituting two new paragraphs for the existing paragraph 4 of Schedule 2. These require information to be provided by education authorities or governing bodies about various aspects of the school curriculum and apply to schools in Wales and England respectively. In the case of schools in England, regulation 3 further amends the 1981 Regulations to provide that where the information is to be published by the local education authority, it shall be supplied to them by the governing body and shall be published without material alteration.

Regulation 4 requires the governing bodies of maintained schools to include in their annual report particulars of the dates of terms and of half-term holidays, and a summary of any changes to information contained in the school prospectus since it was last published. Copies of the report are to be supplied to the head teacher and to the local education authority or, in the case of a grant-maintained school, to the Secretary of State.

Governing bodies are to give head teachers copies of any statements they have made as to their policy on the curriculum; the head teacher is to make them available for inspection by the public (regulation 5).

Regulation 6 requires the head teachers of maintained schools to provide other information relating to the organisation of the curriculum, and regulation 7 requires head teachers to supply on request copies of the documents referred to in regulation 5 and allows for the supply of copy documents containing the information required by regulation 6; a charge not exceeding the cost of supply may be made.

Regulation 8(1) requires the governing bodies of maintained schools (other than grant-maintained schools) to make available to the education authority the statistical information set out in regulation 8(3) by 30th June in each year in respect of the current school year; the head teacher is to make the same information available to the governing body by 30th June in respect of education provision which is intended to be made in the next school year (regulation 8(2)).

Regulation 8(4) requires governing bodies to make the information supplied to them by the head teacher available on request to the education authority and the Secretary of State. Regulation 8(5) imposes a further requirement on governing bodies to supply the education authority with details of pupils without statements of special educational needs for whom the provisions of the National Curriculum have been modified or disapplied, and of pupils with such statements.

The particulars required by regulation 8(1) and (2) are to be in the relevant form set out in Schedule 1, and those required by regulation 8(5) in the relevant form set out in Schedule 2 (regulation 9).

Regulation 10 makes similar provision to regulations 8 and 9 in respect of grant-maintained schools, but provides that the information should be sent to the Secretary of State and, where it relates to pupils with statements of special educational needs, to the education authority.

Regulation 11 provides for the education authority to send the Secretary of State copies of the particulars supplied to them under regulation 8(1) and (5).

Education authorities are required to notify the Secretary of State of new syllabuses of religious education and to make annual returns by 30th September of determinations by their standing advisory councils as to whether the requirement for Christian collective worship is to apply in particular cases (regulation 12).

Regulation 13 contains supplementary provisions relating to the translation of documents. Finally, regulation 14 places a duty on head teachers and governing bodies to supply information to each other where this is necessary for the other to comply with the Regulations.

Useful organisations

For advice on marketing, and dealing with companies:

Chartered Institute of Marketing
Moor Hall, Cookham
Maidenhead, Berkshire SL6 9QH
phone 06285 24922
fax 06285 31382

Further Education Marketing Network
The Staff College, Coombe Lodge
Blagdon, Bristol BS18 6RG
phone 0761 462503
fax 0761 463140

The Marketing Society,
Stanton House, 206 Worple Road
London SW20 8PW
phone 081 879 3464
fax 081 879 0362

National Consumer Council
20 Grosvenor Gardens
London SW1W 0DH
phone 071 730 3469
fax 071 730 0191

General Consumer Council for Northern Ireland
Elizabeth House, 116 Holywood Road
Belfast BT4 1NY
phone 0232 672488
fax 0232 657701

Scottish Consumer Council
314 St Vincent Street
Glasgow G3 8XW
phone 041 226 5261
fax 041 221 0731

Welsh Consumer Council
Castle Buildings, Womanby Street
Cardiff CF1 2BN
phone 0222 396056
fax 0222 238360

For information and advice on sponsorship:

Association for Business Sponsorship of the Arts (ABSA)
Nutmeg House, 60 Gainsford Street
London SE1 2NY
phone 071 378 8143
fax 071 407 7527

For making complaints about unjust or unfair treatment or unwarranted
infringement of privacy by radio or television programmes:

Broadcasting Complaints Commission
Grosvenor Gardens House
35-37 Grosvenor Gardens
London SW1W 0BS
phone 071 630 1966
fax 071 828 7316

For making similar complaints about newspapers or magazines:

Press Complaints Commission
1 Salisbury Square
London EC4Y 8AE
phone 071 353 1248
fax 071 353 8355

References

Association for Business Sponsorship of the Arts' *Principles for Good Practice in Arts Sponsorship*, 1990.

Auld, Robin (Chair), *Report on the Inquiry into William Tyndale School*, Inner London Education Authority, 1976.

Department of Education and Science, *Parental Awareness of School Education, Interpretative Report*, 1989.

Thomas, Michael, *The Economist's Pocket Guide to Marketing*, Basil Blackwell and *The Economist*, 1986.

Education Act 1944, HMSO.

Education (No 2) Act 1986, HMSO.

Education Reform Act 1988, HMSO.

Heller, Robert, *The Pocket Manager*, Hodder and Stoughton, 1986.

Inner London Education Authority Research and Statistics, *Attitudes to School : A Study of the Parents of Third-Year Pupils*, 1986.

Johnson, D. and Ransom, E., 'Parents' Perceptions of Secondary Schools', in Craft, M., Raynor, J., and Cohen, L. (eds), *Linking Home and School*, Harper and Row, 1980.

Family and School, Croom Helm, 1983.

Levi, Primo, *The Periodic Table*, Michael Joseph, 1984.

Macbeth, Alastair, *Involving Parents*, Heinemann Organisation in Schools Series, 1989.

Manser, Martin H., *Printing and Publishing Terms*, Chambers, 1988.

Marland, Michael, 'At Arm's Length' in *Forum*, Volume 7, Number 1, Autumn, 1964.

'Parents, Schooling, and the Welfare of Pupils', in Ribbins, Peter, *Schooling and Welfare*, The Falmer Press, 1985.

Olins, Wally, *The Corporate Personality*, The Design Council, 1978.

Plowden, Lady (Chair), Report of the Central Advisory Council for Education, *Children and their Primary Schools*, HMSO, 1967.

Shipman, Marten, 'The Limits of Positive Discrimination', in Marland, Michael (Editor), *Education for the Inner City*, Heinemann Organisation in Schools Series, 1980.

Shreeve, Robin, Thorp, Jane, and Rickett, John, *Marketing Hertfordshire Colleges*, Herts County Council/Ware College Marketing and Information Unit, 1989.

Taylor, Tom (Chair), *A New Partnership for Our Schools*, being the report of the Taylor Committee, HMSO, 1977.

Index